THE ROBERT HUSSEIN CASE

THE ROBERT HUSSEIN CASE

Its Ramifications for U.S.-Kuwaiti Relations
and International Law

RELIGION AND LAW SERIES, VOLUME SIX

George J. Gatgounis

WIPF & STOCK · Eugene, Oregon

THE ROBERT HUSSEIN CASE
Its Ramifications for U.S.-Kuwaiti Relations and International Law

Religion and Law Series, Volume Six

Copyright © 2022 George J. Gatgounis. All rights reserved. Except for brief quotations in critical publications or reviews, no part of this book may be reproduced in any manner without prior written permission from the publisher. Write: Permissions, Wipf and Stock Publishers, 199 W. 8th Ave., Suite 3, Eugene, OR 97401.

Wipf & Stock
An Imprint of Wipf and Stock Publishers
199 W. 8th Ave., Suite 3
Eugene, OR 97401

www.wipfandstock.com

PAPERBACK ISBN: 978-1-7252-6131-0
HARDCOVER ISBN: 978-1-7252-6132-7
EBOOK ISBN: 978-1-7252-6133-4

VERSION NUMBER 122223

CONTENTS

FOREWORD, BY H. WAYNE HOUSE | xi

PREFACE BY ATTORNEY JOHN WHITEHEAD, THE RUTHERFORD INSTITUTE | xiii

INTRODUCTION | 1
  The Facts of the Robert Hussein Case | 1
    Pre-Conversion to Christianity, as a Kuwaiti Muslim | 2
    Conversion to "Closet" Christianity | 2
    Open Testimony of Conversion to Christianity | 3
    Resultant Sentence of Apostasy | 3
    Trial, Conviction, and Emigration to the U.S. | 5
    Conversion Back to Islam and Return to Kuwait | 6
    Significance of the Case | 6
  The Issues Raised | 7
    To Kuwaiti Constitutional Integrity | 7
    To Current U.S.-Kuwaiti Relations | 7
  Scope and Statement of Thesis | 8
    Delimitations | 8
    Thesis Stated | 9

ORIENTATION: THE INFLUENCE OF ISLAMIC RESURGENCE UPON RECENT DEVELOPMENTS IN INTERNATIONAL LAW | 10
  The Qur'an as a Source of Law and Government | 10
    Qur'anic Law | 10

The Qur'an's Doctrine of Government of Allah | 11
The Qur'an's Prescriptions on the Relation of Islamic Nations with
    Non-Islamic Nations | 12
The Qur'anic Doctrine of "Mosque and State" | 14
Increasing Secularization under the Realities of Statecraft over
    Conquered Peoples | 15
The Islamic Doctrine of Holy War or J'had | 16
The Nebulous Nature of Islamic Political Thought | 17
The Development of an Islamic Orthodoxy | 18
Islamic Law and International Law | 19
The Practical Problems of Imposition of Islamic Law upon
    Nations | 20
Methodological Considerations in Evaluating the Ramifications of
    Islamic Resurgence to International Law | 21
Spheres of Islamic Political Activism | 23
  The Eradication of Western-Imported Legal Systems and the
      Reinstitution of Islamic Law | 23
  Increased Religious Allusion and Symbolism | 24
  Metamorphosis of Social Mores | 25
  Political Activist Organizations | 25
  International Organizations to Promote Unity among Islamic
      Nations | 27
  Educational Reform | 27
The Delicate Balance Moderate Arab States Must Follow in
    Foreign Policy | 28
A Focus on Shiite Activism | 29
A Focus on the Role of Islamic Resurgence in the Foreign
    Policy of Qadhdafi | 30
  The General Pattern of Erosion of Shari'a and Absorption of
      Western Legal Codes | 30
  Qadhdafi's Role of Limiting the Shari'a in Libya | 31
  Qadhdafi's Redefinition of the Divine Law, the Shari'a | 32
  Qadhdafi's Attack on Islamic Shirk or Para-Qur'anic Religious
      Documents | 32
  Qadhdafi's Standing with Shiite Revolutionaries | 34

A Focus on the Iranian Revolution and Its Doctrine of
   International Expansion | 35
   Islam as a Catalyst for International Revolution | 35
   *The International Ramifications of the Rise of Ayatollah
      Khomeini* | 36
   Militant Shia Fueling War with Iraq | 37
   National Statutes Resulting from the Shiite Revolution | 37
The Impact of the Constitution of the Islamic Republic upon
   International Law | 40
International Response to the Iranian Revolution | 42
   The Formation of the Gulf Cooperation Council | 42

THE ISSUE OF KUWAITI CONSTITUTIONAL INTEGRITY:
THE KUWAITI CONSTITUTION PURPORTS TO
GUARANTEE "ABSOLUTE" FREEDOM OF RELIGION | 44
   Distinguishing Real Law from "Window Dressing" | 44
      Dubious Phraseology | 44
      Functional Constitutional Subordination to Islamic Law | 45
         Shari'a as "a Main Source" of Law | 45
         Qur'anic Basis for Statecraft | 46
         The Purpose of the Islamic State | 47
      Subordination to the Ruling Amir | 49
         Real Hope for Peaceful Change Lies in the Amir | 51
   Distinguishing the Kuwaiti Constitution from Conduct,
      "Paper" from Practice | 52
      Feudalistic and Unrepresentative Power Structure | 53
         Gross Human Rights Abuses | 53
   The Analysis of Article 35, "Freedom of Religion Is Absolute,"
      in the Kuwaiti Constitution—Does the Article Have
      Teeth? | 54
      Historical Origins | 54
         The Drafting of Kuwaiti Constitution | 54
      Examples of Constitutional Evolution in the Islamic World | 55
         Before the Twentieth Century | 55
         *Twentieth-Century Examples of Constitutional Evolution in the
            Islamic World* | 56

Western Sources for Article 35 of the Kuwaiti Constitution | 58
Comparison with Similar Provisions in Constitutions of Other
Islamic States | 58
Conclusion | 59

ISLAMIC DIVINE LAW'S (SHARIA) CAPITAL
PUNISHMENT UPON APOSTASY DENIES THE
INALIENABLE HUMAN RIGHT TO CHOOSE ONE'S
BELIEFS | 60

PROPOSED SOLUTIONS TO THE PROBLEM OF
HONORING THE HUMAN RIGHTS OF KUWAITI
MUSLIMS WHO CHANGE THEIR RELIGION | 60
Toward an Islamic Ideological Basis for Religious Toleration
in Kuwait | 60
Qur'anic Passages Implying Religious Totalitarianism | 60
Qur'anic Passages Implying Religious Toleration | 61
A Qur'anic Theology of Toleration | 64
A Summary of the Theology of Toleration in the Qur'an | 64
Pure Qur'anic Theology Does Not Prescribe Capital Punishment
for Muslims Who Change Their Religion | 64
Various Muslim Human-Rights Organizations Seek
Enforcement of the Qur'anic Toleration Passages in Islamic
Countries | 65
Toward Honoring the Ideals of International Conventions in
Kuwait | 67
The Foundational Principle of International Law | 67
Specific International Conventions Codified | 67
United Nations' General Assembly Resolution on the
Declaration for the Elimination of All Forms of Intolerance
and of Discrimination Based on Religion and Belief | 68
An International Consensus, as Represented by International
Declarations, Exists That Choosing One's Religion Is a
Fundamental Right | 71
Toward a Peaceful and Friendly Relationship with the United
States | 79

The Integrity of the U.S.'s Moralistic Claims That Allegedly
        Motivated the Gulf War | 80
The Enforcement of Shari'a's Capital Punishment upon
        Apostates an Obstacle to Full and Friendly Relations
        between the U.S. and Kuwait | 83
Toward a Kuwaiti Relaxation of Religious Exclusivism | 84
    Deconstructing Islamic Provincialism on Human Rights | 84
        The Problem of Cultural Relativism | 84
        *A Negative Precedent: International Convention Declared Null
            and Void by Iran* | 86
        *A Positive Precedent: International Convention Upheld by Law
            in a Muslim State* | 88
    Legislative Proposals to Crack the Door to Religious
        Liberty | 89
        *The Expatriation Option—Non-Muslims Are, Under
            Reasonable Terms, Deported* | 89
        *The Dispatriation Option—Non-Muslims Are No Longer Under
            Religious Law and Judiciaries but Allowed into an Internal
            Apartheid Zone, Designated "International," Allowing for
            Free Speech* | 90

CONCLUSION | 92

FOREWORD, BY H. WAYNE HOUSE

What is freedom, really? Of the many influential religious litigation cases with which my friend, Rev. Dr. George Gatgounis, Esq., has been involved, his work through the esteemed Rutherford Institute as counsel on the Robert Hussein case is certainly one of the most compelling. Through his defense of Hussein, a Kuwaiti citizen sentenced to death by his government for converting to Christianity, Dr. Gatgounis gained a unique vantage point by which his insights were formed and this immensely important work was created.

Robert Hussein's trial was the first of its kind in liberated Kuwait, and correspondingly, this book is the first to expose the ethical ramifications this trial presents regarding United States foreign policy. While many books are concerned with Islamic politics, this work stands out as having particular value as a result of the questions it raises concerning our own U.S. definition of tyranny and the standard by which we judge a government's worthiness to receive U.S. assistance.

By first defining and developing our sense of what constitutes tyranny, we are then led to examine our views of freedom. This work requires nothing less than an honest perspective in doing so, for this is the only hope we have to discern solid answers to questions regarding our own U.S. policies overseas: Did the "liberation" of Kuwait merely grant governmental freedom to enforce its own independent brand of tyranny? Further, how do we rank the ethical priorities of the U.S. government in its decisions to involve or not to involve in world conflicts?

Despite much debate spanning many years, the theories and explanations regarding the motivations that fueled our nation's involvement in the Kuwait-Iraq conflict remain varied and unproven, while its significance remains evident even in our current Middle Eastern relations. Dr. Gatgounis' work is a telling portrait of U.S.-world relations that brings light to questions of foreign religious policies in Kuwait and the Arab world at large, as well as to the ethics and implications of U.S. and international policies regarding the affairs of nations with similar Islamic religious state laws and constitutions.

The American value of freedom against tyranny is the entire basis upon which our nation was founded, and our freedom to worship as we choose is so vitally important that it is protected and maintained through its inclusion in the First Amendment, called the "Bill of Rights," in the U.S. Constitution. Ironically, this guaranteed freedom of religion is also included in the constitution created by Robert Hussein's post-Gulf War "liberated" Kuwait, providing sobering evidence that in the event that a nation's constitution is limited by the tyranny of religious Islamic law, it becomes useless.

Dr. Gatgounis' gift is to provide great depth and insight with equally great clarity, and it is both to his credit and the reader's benefit that he ingeniously offers an understandable argument without ever understating or oversimplifying the complicated dynamic of motives and pressures on Muslim-Christian converts. Instead, this work is a powerful tool with which author and reader together may pierce the growing fog of corruption, sensationalism, sentimentalism, and nationalism that surround such issues, thereby illuminating truth for the good of our nation and our world, in the hope that all may truly understand and experience what freedom is.

H. Wayne House

PREFACE

With the cost of American blood, Kuwait is allegedly "free." But how "free" is "free"? For Robert Hussein, "free" is a relative term—so relative that he may be free to lose his life. Hussein became a Christian in Kuwait and a Kuwaiti court sentenced him to die for it. One of our attorneys, the Rev. Dr. George J. Gatgounis, Esq., helped the International Department of the Rutherford Institute, headed by Pedro Moreno, Esq., to defend the human rights of Mr. Hussein. Here is Hussein's story, with an analysis by attorney Gatgounis of its implications for international law and U.S.-Kuwaiti relations.

Propelling the Rutherford Institute's concern for freedom of religious expression is the belief that conscience is sacred. Allegedly propelling the U.S. military intervention in Kuwait was the ideal of freedom.

Have we as a nation really fought for what we said we did? Is Kuwait really free? Can a Kuwaiti citizen believe what he or she believes to be the truth without persecution? Robert Hussein's story may lead you to believe otherwise.

John Whitehead, The Rutherford Institute

INTRODUCTION

THE FACTS OF THE ROBERT HUSSEIN CASE

The facts of the Robert Hussein case include several phases: pre-conversion to Christianity as a Kuwaiti Muslim before 1991, conversion to "closet" Christianity, open testimony of conversion, resultant sentence for apostasy, emigration to the U.S., and finally conversion back to Islam and return to Kuwait.[1]

---

1. See e.g. *Agence Fr.-Presse*, January 30, 1997, at page unavailable online (explaining Robert Hussein's conversion back to Islam); *Agence Fr.-Presse*, November 26, 1996, page unavailable online; Barbara G. Bake, "Muslim Convert Hussein Flees Kuwait for United States," *Christianity Today*, vol. 40, no. 11, October 7, 1996, p. 88; Michael Coren, "All Things Considered: Kuwait Doesn't Live Up to Its Promise of Religious Freedom: Christian Convert's House Was Attacked, His Wife Assaulted, and Police Refused Protection," *The Financial Post* 17, October 2, 1996, at 1; Tom Carter, World, Briefing/Global Issues, Q&A, "Americans Fail to Share Pain of Those Practicing Same Faith Overseas," *Washington Times*, September 30, 1995, A16; Laurie Goodstein, Metro, Advance Desk, Religion, "Evangelicals Mount Campaign Against Oppression of Christians Protest: Leaders Seek to Elevate Their Cause on Behalf of Those Persecuted Abroad to a National Crusade, Modeled on Efforts to Free Soviet Jews," *Los Angeles Times*, September 30, 1996, A16; Laurie Goodstein, "Religious Persecution Worldwide Prompts Condemnation by the U.S.," *The Courier-Journal* Louisville, KY, September 23, 1996, 04A; Laurie Goodstein, "Evangelical Christians Seek Action; Administration: Congress Reacts to Call to Fight Persecution," *Washington Post*, September 22, 1996, A03.

INTERNATIONAL LAW AFLOAT ON A SEA OF WORLD RELIGIONS

Pre-Conversion to Christianity, as a Kuwaiti Muslim

Hussein Qambar Ali, as he was known prior to his conversion to Christianity, first developed interest in Christianity during his first visit to Philadelphia in 1977. His interest in the new faith derived partially from his interaction with Christians in America.[2] Following this first visit to the United States, Hussein returned to Kuwait and established a successful construction business.

Conversion to "Closet" Christianity

While developing his prosperous business, Hussein prosecuted his interest in Christianity with quietness and discretion. Hussein's interest blossomed into commitment requiring his admission that he was no longer a Muslim in 1984. His muted admission, however, was not made public—Hussein discretely sought out Christian contacts and literature.[3] In 1989, Hussein married but did not communicate his "closet" rejection of Islam and ever-growing interest in Christianity to his wife until after they were married.

Open Testimony of Conversion to Christianity

Their marriage bore fruit—two children were born to Hussein before he completed reading the New Testament in 1993, which reading culminated in his public embrace of Christianity. Motivated by his new faith, Hussein took the Christian name of Robert.

Although Hussein did not publicize his conversion to Christianity, he allowed his immediate family members to become aware of his change. His wife's family, incensed by his "apostasy," disowned Hussein. Estrangement because of his religious conversion intensified, culminating in Hussein's wife leaving him, taking the children with her. She forbad Hussein any visitation rights.

---

2. "Death Sentence: Support Grows for Kuwaiti Christian," *Evangelicals Now* (August 1996), 1, 8.

3. "The Distressing Case of the Kuwaiti Convert Facing the Death Penalty," *Westminster Watch*, July 1996), 9.

INTRODUCTION

Further, her abandonment drew attention to Hussein's changed religious views.

Resultant Sentence of Apostasy

Before Hussein was charged with apostasy, Hussein's wife was raped on grounds that the wife of an apostate has no better standing than a prostitute or slave. Seeking legal redress, Hussein filed suit in a Kuwaiti court demanding visitation rights to see his children. When the reason for his estrangement from his wife became known, the *Kuwaiti Times* sought an interview with Hussein. The interview exposed the reality of Hussein's religious conversion in December 1995.

Hearing of Hussein's unabashed embrace of Christianity, various Kuwaiti attorneys filed suit against him, charging him with apostasy. The attorneys, Abdullah Lattef Al-Asaleh and Mohammad Al-Jaddai, publicly admitted they sought to establish the supremacy of Sharia law in Kuwait, utilizing Hussein's case to set a post-liberation precedent, demonstrating that Western liberation did not mean Western religious declension.[4] In February 1996, a Sunni Family Court refused to hear the case, citing Hussein as one who is no longer under Sunni authority. A Shi'a court saw apostasy as well within its ambit of authority.[5]

Hussein countered, arguing that no religious court, Shi'a or Sunni, should have authority over him in religious adjudication because he was no longer an adherent of either sect of Islam. Hussein pled that since he should not be judged by a religion to which he no longer adhered, fundamental fairness required his trial in a civil court. The Sharia (Islamic divine law) court rebutted, stating that since child custody is a matter under Sharia and that child custody was a direct result of his apostasy, the Sharia court had authority to adjudicate both matters in joinder. Although Hussein pled that Article 35 of the Kuwaiti Constitution states that

4. "Death Sentence," *Evangelicals Now*.

5. Ahmed M. Quraishi, "Robert Protected by Constitution," *Arab Times*, February 12, 1996.

"freedom of religion is absolute," the Sharia court not only denied assignment of the case to a secular court but filed the case to a Sharia court comprised of Shi'a Muslims.

Islamic fundamentalists of both Sunni and Shi'a conviction (of the 50 seats in the Kuwaiti Parliament, four were Shi'a, the remaining Sunni) endeavored to prove religious resolve by applying the death sentence to Hussein. Western influence in Kuwait rising to an all-time high through the military liberation, Islamic reactionaries drew their own proverbial line in the sand.

Islamic fundamentalist recalcitrance flexed its muscle further by engineering the Kuwaiti Amir's appointment of the "Higher Advisory Committee for the Implementation of Sharia." High on the agenda of the Higher Advisory Committee, for instance, was gender discrimination in all Kuwaiti schools. Forced gender discrimination would effect closing of many private schools because of revenue cuts. Public schools in Kuwait are a chief instrument in the Islamic indoctrination of the young.

Trial, Conviction, and Emigration to the U.S.

In January 1996, the Rutherford Institute, alerted to the tragic violation of Hussein's human rights, interceded on his behalf, asking the Amir to respect Hussein's rights as per the Kuwaiti Constitution. The Kuwaiti Embassy responded, "The government of Kuwait respects the rights and religious beliefs of its non-Muslim citizens. ... I can assure you the safety and protection of Mr. Ali [Hussein]." The Rutherford Institute interceded for Hussein before the U.S. Secretary of State, Warren Christopher. Christopher responded that the U.S. Embassy in Kuwait "is closely monitoring this case as a human rights matter, regarding the freedom of religion in Kuwait." U.S. Congressman Frank R. Wolf followed suit, acquiring 15 other Congressperson's signatures in support of Hussein's right to self-determine his religious convictions without penalty.

Despite intercession, however, Islamist lawyers filed in another Kuwaiti court a motion to strip Hussein of any rights as citizen on April 17, 1996. Islamist prosecutors argued that Hussein would

INTRODUCTION

escape sanctions if his case was removed to a Constitutional court, and therefore, religious fidelity demanded his sentence under the original Sharia court. The lead prosecutor against Hussein conceded that there is no body of Kuwaiti political law that requires capital punishment for an apostate. However, the lead prosecutor appealed higher law, arguing that a court, under God, must "follow God's punishment," because the Qu'ran says that whoever changes his religion should be killed. Hussein's defense attorney rebutted that Hussein, as a Kuwaiti citizen, possesses constitutional protection for expression of his beliefs, religion, or opinions. Succumbing to death threats, however, Hussein's defense attorney bowed out of the line of prosecutorial fire. The lead prosecutor posited that Sharia courts in Kuwait need not honor the constitutional guarantees because there is no law above God's. Hence, according to the prosecutor, Sharia courts must apply only Sharia law, Kuwaiti constitutional guarantees notwithstanding. Procedurally, the Sharia court moved so swiftly against Hussein that they denied him any opportunity to speak, and further, any opportunity to read the charges against him before, during, or after the death sentence. Sharia judges reasoned that for an apostate to read the charge, which included citations from the Qu'ran, was akin to outrageous blasphemy. A subsequent hearing on April 24 denied Hussein opportunity to speak in his own defense, holding that Constitutional guarantees do not supersede Islamic Sharia.

Appalled by Hussein's treatment, nine Senators petitioned the Kuwaiti government on May 10, 1996, to protect Hussen's right to self-determine his religious views. On May 23, 1996, eight other Senators drafted and delivered their own letter pleading for the same liberty, including the provision for his legal representation.

Tragically, on May 29, 1996, the Islamic Sharia Court declared Hussein an apostate. The time for its adjudication was approximately thirty seconds. The presiding judge called "obvious" that Article 35 of the Constitution protects all religions but not one who leaves Islam to embrace Christianity. Hussein subsequently fled Kuwait, fearing for his life, to Colorado.

INTERNATIONAL LAW AFLOAT ON A SEA OF WORLD RELIGIONS

Conversion Back to Islam and Return to Kuwait

While residing in Colorado, Hussein, having been unilaterally declared divorced by the Kuwaiti Sharia court, remarried, his new wife having served as a Protestant Christian missionary. On January 30, 1997, however, Reuter's international news agency reported that Hussein had returned to Kuwait, having returned also to Islam. Hussein's new wife, returning with him, stated that she desired to convert to Islam.

Significance of the Case

The significance of the Hussein case is of moment because of the number of countries where the Islamic ideology is hegemonic or at least influential. The countries where Muslims live in appreciable numbers to effect at least a viable, if not hegemonic, political voice include Afghanistan, Albania, Algeria, Bahrain, Bangladesh, Bosnia, Bulgaria, Burma, Cameroon, Chad, China, Dahomey, Egypt, Ethiopia, Fiji, Indonesia, India, Iran, Iraq, Ivory Coast, Jordan, Kuwait, Lebanon, Malaysia, Libya, Maldivie Islands, Mali, Mauritania, Morocco, Niger, Nigeria, Oman, Pakistan, Philippines, Qatar, Saudi Arabia, Senegal, Serbia, Sierra Lenoe, Sudan, Syria Tanzania, Thailand, Togo, Tunisia, Union of Arab Emirates, Upper Volta, various states of the Commonwealth of Independent States, and Yemen.[6] The case is paradigmatic of issues affecting the integrity of international human rights conventions.

THE ISSUES RAISED

To Kuwaiti Constitutional Integrity

Crucial to Kuwaiti constitutional integrity is the enforcement of its Article 35, guaranteeing "absolute" religious freedom. A death

---

6. S. Farooq Hassan, *The Islamic Republic: Politics, Law & Economy* (1984), 61.

INTRODUCTION

sentence for conversion from Islam evidences that shari'a trumps the constitution, and that Kuwait is not a constitutional monarchy. The sentence of apostasy includes not only civil-rights ramifications but also economic. Under all the various schools of traditional Islamic legal theory, a Muslim who "commits apostasy" has no right to their family inheritance unless they convert back to Islam at the time of their father's death. Further, the domestic dimension of an apostasy sentence includes automatic divorce by judicial fiat.[7]

To Current U.S.-Kuwaiti Relations

If the U.S. effort to liberate Kuwait, draped in the rhetoric of liberty, proceeded from more than mere economic grounds, the U.S. is morally obligated to influence Kuwait toward a relaxation of religious exclusivism. A peaceful and friendly relationship between the U.S. and Kuwait requires Kuwaiti courts to recognize liberty of conscience, the principle undergirding the U.S. First Amendment.

SCOPE AND STATEMENT OF THESIS

Delimitations

First, outlining foreign policy for the U.S.-Kuwaiti relationship is outside the ambit of this article. Second, this article is not an exhaustive analysis of the Kuwaiti Constitution, Kuwaiti government, or human-rights record; rather this study focuses on international ramifications of the Islamic shari'a death sentence for Kuwaiti citizens who reject Islam for another religion or for no religion. Third, the burden of this study is exploration of the possibility of religious liberty in Kuwait, not the establishment of any other fundamental right.[8] Fourth, the final segment of this article

---

7. Mumammad Khalid Masud, *Islamic Legal Philosophy: A Study of Abu Ishaq Al-Shatibi's Life and Thought* (1977), 127.

8. This chapter, for instance, does not argue for sodomy as a fundamental human right. Consensual relations among like gender is illegal, to a great

does not attempt to draft legislation for consideration by the Kuwaiti Amir, but rather posits ideas for a solution to the problem of honoring the inalienable human rights of Kuwaiti Muslims who change their religious views.

Thesis Stated

The U.S. should urge the Kuwaiti Amir and Parliament to honor the inalienable human rights of Kuwaiti Muslims who change their religion because the Kuwaiti Constitution purports to guarantee religious freedom and shari'a capital punishment upon apostates denies victims their right to choose their beliefs. Possible solutions to honor the rights of Kuwaiti Muslims who change their religion

---

degree, in the international community, including Kuwait, which adheres to Islamic Shari'a for penal sanctions. See Algeria (§ 338, Penal Code); Armenia (former USSR Penal Code still binding); Azerbaijan (former USSR Penal Code still binding); Bahamas (§§ 390 and 530, Penal Code); Bahrain (Islamic Shari'a), Bangladesh (Islamic Shari'a), Belarus (former USSR Penal Code still binding); Bermuda (§ 175, Penal Code); Bosnia-Herzegovina (§ 93.2, Penal Code), Burkina Faso (§ 331, Penal Code); Chile (Art. 365, Penal Code), Cook Islands (§§ 206, 207, Penal Code); Ecuador (Art., Penal Code), Ethiopia (§§ 600, 601, Penal Code), Fiji Islands (§§ 168, 170, Penal Code), Georgia (former USSR Penal Code still binding), Guyana (§§ 351, 353, Criminal Law Offenses Act); India (§ 377, Penal Code); Iran (Arts. 139–156, Penal Code), Jamaica (§§ 76–79, Penal Code); Kiribati (§ 153, Penal Code), Kyrgyzstan (Art. 112, Criminal Code); Libya (§ 407, P 4, Penal Code); Moldova (former USSR Penal Code still binding); Morocco (§ 489, Penal Code), Mozambique (§§ 70, 71, Penal Code); Nicaragua (Art. 204, Penal Code); Nigeria (Arts. 214, 217, Penal Code); Niue (§§ 170, 171, Penal Code); Pakistan (§ 377, Penal Code); Qatar (Islamic Shari'a); Romania (Art. 200, Criminal Code); Saudi Arabia (Islamic Shari'a); Serbia (§ 110.3, Penal Code; § 81.2, Penal Code of Kosovo); Singapore (§ 377, Penal Code); Solomon Islands (§ 153, Penal Code); Sri Lanka (§ 365a, Penal Code); Syria (§ 520, Penal Code); Tanzania (§§ 154–57, Penal Code); Tonga (§ 126, Penal Code); Turkmenistan (former USSR Penal Code still binding); Uganda (§ 140, Penal Code); United States (illegal in over 20 states); Uzbekistan (former USSR Penal Code still binding); Yemen (Islamic Shari'a); Western Somoa (§ 58a, Crimes Ordinance of 1961); Zaire (§§ 168, 169, 170, 172, Penal Code). See generally, James D. Wilets, "International Human Rights Law and Sexual Orientation," *HASTINGS INT'L. & COMP. L. REV.* 1 (Fall, 1994): 18 (claiming sodomy is a human right).

INTRODUCTION

include expatriation or depatriation into an international apartheid zone allowing the free exchange of ideas.

ORIENTATION

The Influence of Islamic Resurgence upon Recent Developments in International Law

To ascertain the particulars of the Robert Hussein case, a general bird's eye view of the effect of Islamic fundamentalist resurgence on international law places the case in its broader perspective.

THE QUR'AN AS A SOURCE OF LAW AND GOVERNMENT

Qur'anic Law

The Qur'an is not only the Islamic holy book, it serves as a quasi-constitution and main source of law. The Qur'an is replete with law that applies both in the religious realm and the civil realm. The scope of its legal precepts include the spiritual and the political.[1] For instance, Sura 7:47–48 establish a *lex talionis*, or standard of justice for any court acting in the name of Islam to apply:

> It was We who revealed
> The Law (to Moses): therein
> Was guidance and light.

---

1. For an example of commentary on the Quran, see generally Abu Ja'far Muhammad B. Jarir al-Tabari, *The Commentary on the Quran* (Oxford: Oxford University Press, 1978).

By its standard have been judged
The Jews, by the Prophets
Who bowed (as in Islam)
To God's Will, by the Rabbis
And the Doctors of Law:
For to them was entrusted
the protection of God's Book,
And they were witnesses thereto:
Therefore fear not men,
But fear Me, and sell not
My Signs for a miserable price.
If any do fail to judge
By (the light of) what God
Hath revealed, they are
(No better than) Unbelievers.

We ordained therein for them:
"Life for life, eye for eye,
Nose for nose, ear for ear,
Tooth for tooth, and wounds
Equal for equal." But if
Any one remits the retaliation
By way of charity, it is
An act of atonement for himself.
And if any fail to judge
By (the light of) what God
Hath revealed, they are
(No better than) wrong-doers.[2]

In the latter verse, the "eye for eye" standard is interpreted as a just retribution for any wrongdoing unless the wrongdoer undertakes some charity to atone for the wrongdoing.

The Qur'an's Doctrine of Government of Allah

The sovereignty of Allah is an all-inclusive concept in the Qur'an. Because Allah is sovereign, Muslims must obey or else be chastised by his hand. In a political sense, the "government of Allah" implies

2. Abdulla Yusuf Ali, *Translation of the Meanings of the Holy Quran* (Beirut: Khalil Al-Rawaf, 1961), 256–58.

that the government of the Islamic nation does not belong to the people but to Allah. As Abdulla Yusuf Ali, a scholarly defender of Islam, argues:

> The concept of "sovereignty of God," in its turn, ensures political equality for all—the rulers and the ruled, and provides the basis for immunizing society from political tyranny. The sovereignty of God can be challenged only by atheists. But even in secular political philosophy, which projects the concept of the "sovereignty of the people," the term "people" stands for a corporation and a conceptual entity as it embraces the past, the present and the future generations of the people of the nation-state, bound all the time by the fundamental principle of a constitution established by the "founding fathers." Thus, there too, it is a "transcendental" entity in which sovereignty is affirmed. However, the antimony that emerges in affirming that the people are "sovereign" and "subject" at the same time created difficulties, which are avoided most rationally in affirming God a *sovereign* and the people as *subjects*.[3]

The Qur'an's Prescriptions on the Relation of Islamic Nations with Non-Islamic Nations

The Qur'an articulates strict prescriptions against association with "Christians" and "Jews." The Qur'anic strictures would include treaties with Christians and Jews. Qur'an 8:54–56 prohibits Muslims from making treaties with Christians and Jews, and promises "ruin" for those Muslims who enter protective treaties with Christians and Jews:

> O ye who believe!
> Take not the Jews
> And the Christians
> For your friends and protectors:

---

3. Muhammad Fazl-Ur-Rahman Ansari, *The Qur'ranic Foundations and Structure of Muslim Society* (Karachi: Indus Educational Foundation, n.d.), 193.

ORIENTATION

> They are but friends and protectors
> To each other. And he
> Amongst you that turns to them
> (For friendship) is of them.
> Verily God guideth not
> A people unjust.
>
> Those in whose hearts
> Is a disease—thou seest
> How eagerly they run about
> Amongst them, saying:
> "We do fear lest a change
> Of fortune bring us disaster."
> Ah! perhaps God will give
> (Thee) victory, or a division
> According to His Will.
> Then will they repent
> Of the thoughts which they secretly
> Harboured in their hearts.
>
> And those who believe
> Will say: "Are these
> The Men who swore
> Their strongest oaths by God,
> That they were with you?"
> All that they do
> Will be in vain,
> And they will fall
> Into (nothing but) ruin.

Clearly, the Qur'an not only negatively prohibits "friendship" with Christians and Jews, it positively prescribes "friendship" with Muslims only. As the following text, 8:58–59 of the Qur'an, states, "real friends" of the Muslim are only God and other Muslims:

> Your (real) friends are
> (No less than) God,
> His Apostle, and the (Fellowship
> Of) Believers,—those who
> Establish regular prayers
> And regular charity,
> And they bow

Down humbly (in worship).

And to those who turn
(For friendship) to God,
His Apostle, and the (Fellowship
Of) Believers,—it is
The Fellowship of God
That must certainly triumph.[4]

The Qur'anic Doctrine of "Mosque and State"

To the Qur'an, there is no separation between the religious body and the political body. There is no line of distinction; the two are one entity. At the inception of Islam, the prophet was both spiritual leader and military leader. Religious and political realms are distinct:

> Islam thus evolved differently from Judaism and Christianity, the other monotheistic faiths which existed in Arabia and the surrounding lands and which were mentioned many times in the divine relations. . . . In the case of Islam, religion was the state—with its Prophet acting as the military commander, making war and peace, collecting taxes, laying down the law and dispensing justice. In contrast, Christ made a distinction between what belonged to God and what belonged to Caesar at the very outset. Since Christianity recognized two separate authorities—Church and State—existing sometimes in harmony and sometimes in conflict.

Judaism, however, does not maintain such a strict distinction between its religious organization and its political organization. But there is, however, a prophet/priest distinction in the Hebrew Scriptures. Further, in the Hebrew Scriptures, the king could not perform priestly duties, and any who tried, like Saul, Israel's first king, were divinely punished. As the Islamic scholar Hiro remarks:

---

4. Ali, 261.

As for Judaism, the situation is unclear: classical rabbinical Judaism emerged only after the Hebrew state had ceased to exist. Judaism, therefore, falls uneasily between Islam and Christianity as far as relations between the state and religion are concerned.[5]

The Constitution of Medina is an enlightening example of the Qur'anic relation between religious and political realms. In A.D. 627, this epic constitution laid the foundation for the Islamic *umma* and the *Dar al Islam*, the Realm of Islam. The Constitution of Medina first established a solid united Islamic community composed of believers and their dependents, the *umma*. The *umma* was subdivided into clans or subdivisions which were individually responsible for blood money and ransoms. The members of the *umma* must show solidarity against crime. *Umma* members were not allowed to give respite to a criminal even if the criminal was a near kinsman. Further, both in war and peace, the Muslims composing the *umma* must maintain solidarity. In case of a dispute between the *umma* members, the dispute would be settled by Allah and Muhammad.[6] The solidarity of the *umma* is maintained by the five pillars of Islam. The pillars of Islam are a matrix of individual and social obligations: *shadith* (saying), *shahada* (act of religious witness), *salat* (prayer), *sakat* (purification), *sawm* (the annual fast of Ramadon) and *hajr* (the holy flight or pilgrimage to Mecca).[7]

Increasing Secularization under the Realities of Statecraft over Conquered Peoples

The Muslim state began as an aspiring theocracy, with a worldview that all nations should be converted to Islam either by persuasion or by the sword and that all nations would be ruled by the Qur'an. However, the realities of international politics produced an

5. Dilip Hiro, *Holy Wars: The Rise of Islamic Fundamentalism* (New York: Routledge, 1989), 9.
6. Ali, 8.
7. Ali, 10.

increasing secularization of the Muslim adherents. After the death of Muhammad, his surviving cousin and nephew were supplanted by a Mu'awiya, who took the reins of the Muslim state. Mu'awiya was far more realistic than the religiously idealistic Muhammad and his cousin and nephew. Mu'awiya introduced the art of Byzantine statecraft using a judicial structure similar to the Byzantine model. As cunning, intrigue, and corruption began to infect the courts of the Muslim cleric-judges, the theocratic worldview gave way to the painful and mundane realities of maintaining power over conquered peoples. Islam began to absorb the Persian wisdom of statecraft through the apt Arab pupils of Persian viziers. A Persian convert to Islam, Ibn al-Muqaffa', was a secretary in the court of both the Omayyads and the first of the Abbasids of Persia prior to their fall to Islam, and he translated into Arabic the Persian Pahlavi, the royal chronicles and court manuals of Sassanian Iran.[8]

The Islamic Doctrine of Holy War or J'had

Islamic law has a violent and militarily aggressive dimension. At least 78 times the Qur'an refers to Holy War or J'had.[9] The Holy War is an incremental part of Islamic international political thought. An Islamic nation committing a wanton act of aggression against an infidel nation may be appear immoral by Western moral and political standards, but the Qur'an condones, even commends, such aggression. The Qur'an promises divine assistance to those Muslims who endeavor national conversion by means of force (3:11, 111, 112, 122–26; 8:9–12, 17, 42–44, 126; 9:25–27; 35:25, 27).[10] War and religion are combined in the passages on J'had.

But to enjoy Allah's assistance in battle, the Islamic army must submit to Allah's regulations and rules of J'had (4:71, 94, 104; 5:33, 34). Islamic warriors were to pray constantly for victory (4:101–3).

    8. Arthur J. Arberry, *Aspects of Islamic Civilization as Depicted in the Original Texts* (London: George Allen and Unwin, Ltd., 1964), 14–15.

    9. *Subject-Wise Index to the English Koran* (Karachi: Peermahomed Ebrahim Trust, 1973).

    10. Ibid., 63.

ORIENTATION

The Qur'an serves to inspire Muslims to fight against infidels. Muslims are roused and encouraged for Holy War in a wide variety of passages (2:19–97, 216, 244; 3:120–27, 138, 164–167, 194; 4:35, 74–77, 84; 8:39, 40, 46, 59, 60, 65, 66; 9:29). Further, the Qur'an excoriates any Muslim who through cowardice shrinks back from going into battle (4:75, 95; 9:38, 43, 83; 33:13–20). The historical sections of the Qur'an include at least 242 verses on the various battles of Muhammad (Ahzab or Khandaq, 33:9–25; Badar, 3:13, 123–24, 163–67; Badar-e-Sughra, 5:83, 84; Bani Mustalaq, 63:1–8; Bani Saleem, 100:1–5; Khaiber, 48:27; Hunain, 9:25–27; Tabuk, 9:38–123; Uhud, 3:121, 122, 125–129, 139, 140, 164–79; Destruction of Bani Quraizah, 33:26, 27; Exile of bani Nuzeer, 59:2–6; Sirreyyah of Abdullah Bin Jahash, 2:217; Hudaibyyah and Baite-Rezwan, 48:4, 18; forecast of Victory of Mecca, 48:27).[11] The Qur'an produces an aggressive nationalist fortress mentality, viewing the gains of Islam as non-negotiable and what is not Islam as a target for aggression.

The Islamic Republic of Pakistan is a direct result of a national revolt inspired by the vision of an Islamic international order. Iqbal, like his Islamic fellow revolutionaries before him since the eighth century, dreamed of a "world united in glad acceptance of the challenge of Islam, the challenge to man and men to make themselves sharers with God in the creation of a perfect and perfectly self-realizing Universe."[12] J'had is one means to attain this end.

The Nebulous Nature of Islamic Political Thought

Islamic political thought is not a well-defined complex of propositions. Rather, Islamic political thought is composed of "generalities, broad statements of goals and a vague conception of a constitutive process."[13] The general formulation of pure Islamic

---

11. Ibid., 22–23.
12. Ibid., 381.
13. M.H.A. Reisman, "Islamic Fundamentalism and Its Impact on International Law and Politics," in *The Influence of Religion upon the Development of*

theory, as espoused by the resurgent fundamentalists, is simple theocracy. God's will is superior to everyone else's. The will of the majority is irrelevant if that will contradicts the divine will. A rule of the people, by the people, and for the people is therefore foreign to a pure Islamic government. Since the divine will is the crux of the Islamic political theory, those who have devoted their entire lives to finding God and knowing his mind are those who have the right to rule.[14] The model Islamic state is one ruled by the religious clerics according to the Qur'an. Lawyer-clerics are Allah's mouthpiece to the Islamic community, communicating the all-important will of Allah.

The Development of an Islamic Orthodoxy

When Islam began its career of conquest, it had "no theology and very little law so that within wide limits every man did that which was right in his own eyes."[15] During the first three centuries of Islam, the body of orthodox Islamic opinion divided into two categories, each with its own adherents.[16] The Sunni held that Qur'an and the body of commentary surrounding it and the life of Muhammad were the final and complete revelations of Allah. Therefore, no Muslim cleric could add to that revelation from Allah. The Shia branch held that specially inspired imams, or prophets, could be raised up by Allah to communicate Allah's will to his people. These prophets could not contradict the Qur'an but could add to it by providing specific guidance to Allah's people.

International Law (Dordrecht: Martinus Nijhoff Publishers, 1991), 116.

14. Ibid., 117.

15. A.S. Tritton, *Muslim Theology* (Bristol: Luzac and Company, Ltd.: 1947), 9.

16. Ibid.

ORIENTATION

Islamic Law and International Law

Islamic fundamentalism is a core ideology that grows in the number of its adherents. This ideology tends to oppose Westernization and revisionism of historic Islamic ideology and tradition. The growth of Islamic fundamentalism is a major phenomenon. As Ismail Seragedlin, a modern scholar of Arab studies, notes:

> The Arab world today is in the throes of a major, though subtle, upheaval. Everywhere, in every Arab country, a rekindling of interest in religion and religious affairs is noticeable. In some cases this takes the form of the resurgence of militant political Islamic fundamentalism. In other cases, it takes the form of overt zealotry and adherence to patterns of ritual, dress, and behavior associated with medieval Muslim societies, even when many of these patterns of behavior contain little if anything that is inherently Islamic. Examples of this behavior would be growing of beards (inspired by prophetic lore), the wearing of certain clothes among women, and even the refusal of some of the more fervent young zealots to sleep on beds.[17]

Actually, the Prophet Muhammad predicted "at the turn of each century there will arise in my nation a man who will call for a religious revival."[18] The goal of the Islamic fundamentalist resurgence is the conversion of *anomie*. Anomie is that state in which "normative standards of conduct and belief are weak or lacking and is commonly characterized by disorientation, anxiety, and isolation."[19] The standard to which each state must conform in order to overcome *anomie* is the Divine Law in the Qur'an. The Divine Law is not provincial and limited to Muslims only. All nations are subject to the Islamic law. Therefore, when Islamic fundamentalists call for imposition of the Divine Law, the very imposition has inherent international implications. The teleology of Islam,

17. Ali E. Hillal Dessouki, *Islamic Resurgence in the Arab World* (New York: Praeger Publishers, 1982), 54.
18. Dessouki, introduction.
19. Dessouki, 55.

like the teleology of Marxist-Leninism, is universal conformity to their ideological strictures. Accordingly, national conversion to Islam, whether more extreme Shiite fundamentalism or more moderate Sunni, is viewed as another beachhead to advance upon the entire globe.[20]

The Practical Problems of Imposition of Islamic Law upon Nations

The traditional Western safeguards of human liberty eclipse into insignificance in the face of Islamic legal reformation.[21] Those who would impose the Islamic Divine Law see that law as superhuman. The kind of regime the Islamic proponents desire is "too good for most human beings."[22] Butterworth, the Islamic authority from the University of Maryland, sees the Divine Law standard like the political morality espoused by Socrates' speech on the model city in Plato's *Republic*. Socrates saw the moral standards of his model city as practically unattainable in the here and now.[23] However, those standards espoused by Socrates for the model state were to be goals and ideals to which the developing state, however laden with human imperfections, must strive.

Principles, of course, are necessary for any social order; but the practical means of imposing such principles are the only criteria by which any society can determine the expedience of any particular proposal for reform. Principles in the non-phenomenal realm are of little use in solving the complex issues facing any society unless those principles can put on shoe leather, touch the ground, and direct a society toward betterment. For instance, the

---

20. "Lecture on Teaching and Learning," in *An Islamic Response to Imperialism: Political and Religious Writings of Sayyid Jamal Al-Din "al-Afghani,"* trans. Nikki R. Keddie (Berkeley: University of California Press, 1968), 101–05, 107.

21. Charles E. Butterworth, "Prudence Versus Legitimacy," in *Islamic Resurgence in the Arab World*, (New York: Praeger Publishers, 1982), 109.

22. Ibid., 110.

23. Plato, *Republic*, trans. Paul Shorey (Cambridge, Mass.: Harvard University Press, 1963), 500ff.

social principle of *Ijmac*, or agreement between citizens, rings true in virtually any society, whether theistic, atheistic, or pluralistic.[24] The principle, simply stated, is that a society should take on no initiative, to use Lyndon Johnson's oft-repeated pat phrase, unless "there appears to be a consensus." Such a principle rings true from even common logic. As Jesus stated, "a kingdom divided against itself cannot stand." Lenin repeated the obverse of the principle when he predicted the division of the West, and its division and devouring by the Eastern bloc. But, how is one to implement the principle? Should democracies therefore be as pure as possible, where every contingency is placed to a referendum, as far as administrative burdens will allow? Or, does *Ijmac* require only that referenda be held only in the form of free elections? On what issues should elected officials turn to popular referenda, or are opinion polls the best fulfillment of the *Ijmac* requirement? As long as such principles remain non-phenomenal with no procedural dimension, such principles will do little good outside a merely academic environment. The Islamic principles, however idealistically noble, must have a concrete procedural dimension in order to be valuable realistically. At some point, ideas, in order to useful, must become practical.

Methodological Considerations in Evaluating the Ramifications of Islamic Resurgence to International Law

The phenomenon of the Islamic resurgence has received increasing attention from sociohistorical academia, the media, and the governments threatened by such resurgence. The Islamic resurgence seeks replacement of Western imported legal systems with Qur'an-based social mores, statutes, and judiciaries. Various terms, including "revivalism," "revitalization," "upsurge," reassertion," "renewal," "awakening," "fundamentalism," "neofundamentalism," "resurgence," "militant Islam," and "political Islam," have described the new phenomenon. The increasing activism in the

---

24. Butterworth, 110.

name of Islam demands analysis. Often however, an analysis of such activism degenerates into sensationalism. The media, in its ever-urgent quest for captivating news, finds a "the Muslims are coming!" attitude enticing. Images of the Islamic hordes laying siege to Vienna conjure greater interest by the media's clientele.[25] *Newsweek*, for instance, referred to the resurgence as "Islam on the march."[26]

Another tendency in the attention the Islamic resurgence receives by the Western media is retrogression. Often the Islamic resurgence is viewed as a reaction to the inevitable evolution of societies away from a religious orientation. The new dogmatism is viewed as a reaction to the toleration of divergent secular views fostered by modernity. The new political resolve is viewed as religious extremism. Religious revivalism is considered an anachronism in a scientific age. To reviews of the Islamic resurgence with such an aura, religion and sociology are separate disciplines and the designation of social issues such as the rights of women and the freedom of (secular) expression as religious ones is out of whack.[27]

Yet other treatments of the contemporary Islamic resurgence exhibit actual denial of the nature of the resurgence. One aspect of the denial is that all forms of the resurgence are rigidly uniform. Admittedly, the various elements of the resurgence agree in that the Islamic Divine Law or *shari'a* should be applied universally. However, elements of the resurgence differ in attitude, social context, self-definition, political allegiance and activism, and immediate objectives. Further, adherents of the new resurgence may themselves deny a "newness" at all to the resurgence. Adherents

25. Ali E. Hillal Dessouki, "The Islamic Resurgence: Sources, Dynamics, and Implications," in *Islamic Resurgence in the Arab World*, (New York: Praeger Publishers, 1982), 4–5.

26. *Newsweek*, December 5, 1977, 58–59.

27. Similarly, irreligious elements in the Western press may disdain any form of Christian resurgence evidenced in the 1980, 1984, 1988, and even 1992 U.S. presidential elections and the pro-life movement. Johannes Fabian, "The Anthropological of Religious Movements from Explanation to Interpretation" *Social Research* 46 (1979): 4ff.; James Fernandez, "On the Notion of Religious Movement," *Social Research* 46 (1979): 36ff.

ORIENTATION

claim that the "new" resurgence is merely the numerical and spiritual growth of the old historic Islam.[28] The resurgence, to them, is not new but rather an expansion of what was already there in embryonic form.

SPHERES OF ISLAMIC POLITICAL ACTIVISM

The Eradication of Western-Imported Legal Systems and the Reinstitution of Islamic Law

Islamic political activism manifests in six particular categories. First, in the legal realm, Islamic activists move to eradicate Western-imported legal systems and reinstitute Islamic law. More pronounced expressions of the movement away from generally accepted Western legal standards include the penal amputations according to the Divine Law or *shari'a* in Libya and Mauritania and public flogging of malefactors in Abu Dhabi.[29] In 1971, Egypt included *shari'a* as a source for constitutional and legislative law. Eight years later the *shari'a* was made the sole source for legislation.[30] Three years later the Egyptian parliament passed legislation forbidding any Muslim from imbibing beverage alcohol publicly. Further, the law forbad the sale of beverage alcohol in public areas other than those zones specifically designated as tourist zones. In 1978, Mauritania determined that *shari'a* should be applied to all its domains and that pre-existing legislation must be revised accordingly. The purpose of such legislative reform was to re-affirm Mauritania's "original identity."[31] Sudan established a government committee to examine options to amend their constitution to conform to *shari'a* in 1978.[32]

---

28. Ali E. Hillal Dessouki, "The Islamic Resurgence: Sources, Dynamics, and Implications," in *Islamic Resurgence in the Arab World*, (New York: Praeger Publishers, 1982), 5.
29. Dessouki, 10.
30. Dessouki, 11.
31. *Arab Report and Record* (June 16–30, 1978): 444.
32. Andrew Lycett, "The Great Islamic Revival," in *Arabia and the Gulf*, no.

23

INTERNATIONAL LAW AFLOAT ON A SEA OF WORLD RELIGIONS

Increased Religious Allusion and Symbolism

A second sphere of manifestation of Islamic political activism is religious allusion and symbolism. In Egypt for instance, Sadat was generally known as the "believing president" or *al-ra'is al-mu'min*. Almost all of Sadat's speeches concluded with a religious allusion or quotation. Further, to boost his political agenda, Sadat often referred to his opposition as unbelievers, especially if they were socialistic leftists. *Anathema* became a key buzz word to label his political opponents. The 1973 war against Israel was code named Badr, a key battle of the Prophet Muhammad. Previously, Nassar in Egypt received forceful criticism from Jordan, Saudi Arabia, and Yemen for importing "atheistic" socialism in 1961–64. In 1975, North Yemen established a watchdog department, the first its kind, to monitor the "imported ideologies which oppose Islamic teachings and traditions."[33] Even the ancillary influence of the tourist trade became a target of "Islamization" in Kuwait. In 1978, Kuwait imposed strict restrictions on dancing shows in hotels and nightclubs. The name of art could be used to cloak anti-Islamic practices that "violate the Islamic structure of Kuwait."[34]

Further, more moderate Arab leaders reflected more sensitivity to the changing religious scene by paying more attention to strengthening Islamic sentiment. The most secular of Arab leaders, Bourguiba, started to throw sops to the Islamic right by appeasing and cooperating with their political spokespersons. Bourguiba even gave speeches in the pulpits of the two most influential mosques, Zaytuna and Qayrawan.[35] Mohammar Qahdhafi propagated a unique brand of Islam to bolster his political power base.[36]

---

21 (May 28, 1979): 8–9.

33. *Arab Report and Record* (August 1–15, 1975): 530.

34. *Arabia and the Gulf*, no. 46 (November 13, 1978): 5.

35. Ali E. Hillal Dessouki, "The Islamic Resurgence: Sources, Dynamics, and Implications," in *Islamic Resurgence in the Arab World*, (New York: Praeger Publishers, 1982), 11.

36. Ibid.

ORIENTATION

Metamorphosis of Social Mores

A third sphere of manifestation of rising Islamic sentiment is the realm of social mores. An increasing number of young men wear their beards in traditional Islamic manner. An increasing number of educated younger women wear modest apparel in a way that has been uncommon for decades. The traditional women's apparel leaves only the face and hands uncovered.[37] Surveys conducted in Tunisia in 1967 and 1973 revealed a definite increase in personal religious practices, including the observance of total abstinence from beverage alcohol. Abstainers increased from 46 percent to 73 percent and attendance at religious events increased from 18 percent to 61 percent.[38]

Political Activist Organizations

The fourth sphere of manifestation of Islamic activism is the increase of political opposition organizations. In Egypt for example, four militant Islamic organizations have emerged. The Muslim Brothers Association circulates a monthly magazine called *al-Dacwa*, or "call." This periodical draws heavy criticism from the Egyptian government. Three underground militant groups also appear on the Egyptian political horizon. *Jamacat al-Takfir wa'l-Hijra* (Repentance and Holy Flight), *Shabab Muhammad* (Muhammad's Youth), and *Jund Allah* (God's Soldiers) are currently alive and well as underground sociopolitical dissenting groups.[39]

Further, the Islamic resurgence has borne fruit on university campuses. Student organizations known as *al-Jamaca al-Islamiya* (the Islamic Association) exist at every university. By the late 1970s the *al-Jamaca al-Islamiya* had become the "strongest and cohesive

---

37. Dessouki, 11-12.

38. M.A. Tessler, "Political Change and the Islamic Revival in Tunisia," *Maghreb Review* 5 (1980): 14-15.

39. Ali E. Hillal Dessouki, "The Islamic Resurgence: Sources, Dynamics, and Implications," in *Islamic Resurgence in the Arab World*, (New York: Praeger Publishers, 1982), 12.

political force on Egyptian campuses."[40] These student groups cry out for the application of *shari'a*. Most of the demonstrations against the Shah's residence in Egypt were instigated and manned by religious students. The agitation of the student dissent reached such proportions in May of 1980 that Sadat ordered all student religious societies disbanded. The ban instituted by Sadat was justified as a remedy to "religious fanaticism, extremism, and communal strife."[41]

Some Islamic dissenters have congregated around Muslim preachers. The two most charismatic mosque preachers were Sheikh Muhammed al-Ghazali and Sheikh Kishk. Thousands would flock to hear the Friday Khutbas of these dynamic preachers. Eventually, the former was removed from his post. The latter's sermons are taped and sold commercially in bulk. His appeal is largely emotional and borders on the sensational.[42]

In Algeria, Tunisia, the Gaza strip, and Sudan, Islamic activism has surfaced in force. The Tunisian government responded with both restrictive and conciliatory actions. Government spokesmen in Tunisia criticized Islamic activists of "reviving fanaticism and obscurantism."[43] For three months in 1979, the Tunisian government banned the activist Islamic *al-Mujtmac* (Society). To conciliate the activists, however, the Tunisian government restricted the hours of public beverage alcohol consumption in 1980. Further, the government revoked licenses to bars in the capital. In Algeria, public demonstration by Islamic activists included the public humiliation of El-Oued prostitutes, liquor stores were ransacked in rioting, and in Algiers, the capital, and Oran demonstrators demanded reform in education.[44] Peaceful demonstrations oc-

40. Ibid.
41. Ibid.
42. Ibid.
43. Patrick Blum, "Islamic Revival Fuels Maghreb Discontent," *Middle East Economic Digest* 23 (November 1979): 5–7.
44. *Middle East Newsletter* 130 (December 7, 1979–January 13, 1980): 10–11.

curred in Ouargla, Biskra, and Touggourt.[45] In 1980, Palestinian activists burned liquor stores, movie theaters, and other businesses providing entertainment.[46] In Sudan, the 300—member National Assembly included 60 representatives who were Muslim Brothers.[47]

International Organizations to Promote Unity among Islamic Nations

The fifth sphere of manifestation of Islamic activism is the proliferation of international organizations to promote political and economic relations between Islamic states.[48] Pan-Islamic sentiment fuels several organizations that seek to foster stronger political and economic ties, even political union, between Islamic states. Some of these organizations seek union of all Arabs into a pan-Arabic state united by ethnic, cultural, and religious commonality. Other organizations seek union of all Islamic nations, including Pakistan, Indonesia, and Turkey into a colossal Islamic state bound in religious solidarity.[49]

Educational Reform

A sixth sphere of manifestation of Islamic activism is education. In 1977, the first international conference on Islamic education was

---

45. *Middle East Newsletter* 130 (January 28–February 10, 1980): 4.

46. Dessouki, 13.

47. Ibid.

48. For a discussion of Quranic banking, prohibitions on usury, and legitimate profit, see generally Nabil A. Saleh, *Unlawful Gain and Legitimate Profit in Islamic Law* (Cambridge: Cambridge University Press, 1986). Iran, for instance, has established two Quranic state-supported banks that offer loans without interest.

49. Ali E. Hillal Dessouki, "The Islamic Resurgence: Sources, Dynamics, and Implications," in *Islamic Resurgence in the Arab World*, (New York: Praeger Publishers, 1982), 13.

held in Saudi Arabia.⁵⁰ Forty countries participated and approved an initiative to adopt "an education policy that is based on Islamic outlook and that derives its principles from Islamic sources."⁵¹ The conference focused specifically on the methodology of teaching the sciences. Islam sees any gap between religions and science as purely artificial. The conference therefore recommended a plan to "close the artificial gap between religion and science which was imported along with European methodology."⁵² Consequently, both Tunisia and Algeria reformed their public-school curricula to increase Islamic studies.⁵³

THE DELICATE BALANCE MODERATE ARAB STATES MUST FOLLOW IN FOREIGN POLICY

The following quotation from the Arab scholar Dessouki demonstrates the tightrope upon which the ruling family of the Saudi Arabian kingdom must walk to balance international relations and domestic policy:

> The Saudi ruling class faces a difficult choice. To the extent that it keeps the symbols of the traditional bases of legitimacy—tribe and religion—alive, the more it remains vulnerable to the challenge of Islamic orthodoxy. If, on the other hand, it moves to establish a new basis of legitimacy, it will be eroding its own position and privileges. Here lies the dilemma: the royal family cannot keep the traditional structure of social and political relations unchanged, nor is it ready to accept the eventual consequences of social change, nor is it ready to accept the eventual consequences of social change, particularly those related to political participation. A delicate balance was established in the 1960s by King Faial and was made more effective in the 1970s by the oil wealth. But

---

50. *Arabia and the Gulf*, no. 21 (May 22, 1978): 9.
51. Ibid.
52. Ibid.
53. Dessouki, 12.

the divergence between a rapidly changing society and its political structure remains.[54]

A FOCUS ON SHIITE ACTIVISM

The Shiite branch of the Islamic world has taken the posture of the shock troopers for Allah. Demonstrations, assassination attempts, and political maneuvers have evidenced the resurgence of this branch of Islam and its consequent disdain of imported Western ideology, business, and culture. The Shiite community in Saudi Arabia numbers at least 250,000 and is largely domiciled in the oil-rich eastern province. Demonstrations increase, especially in response to the Saudi link with the United States, the supporter of Israel. On the Ashura feast day in 1980, for instance, riots erupted during the celebration of the martyrdom of al-Husayn ibn Ali in November of 1979.[55] In Iraq, Shiite demonstrations turned violent as early as 1977 in the holy cities of Najaf and Karbala. The Mujahidin, a militant Shiite group, claimed responsibility for the failed assassination attempt on Tariq Aziz, the most senior Christian in the Iraqi government. Saddam Hussein reacted with the immediate execution of Ayatollah Baqir al-Sadr, the ranking Shiite figure in Iraq. In Kuwait, for instance, the government deported the personal representative of the Ayatollah Khomeini, Hojatollislam Abba al-Muhri, his son, and their associates, even though some were Kuwaiti citizens. In November 1979 Kuwaiti Shiites marched on the U.S. embassy but were dispersed by tear gas.[56] In Lebanon, Imam Musa al-Sadr founded the "movement of the deprived," a Shiite activist organization which includes a military unit, *amal*, or "hope."[57]

---

54. Ali E. Hillal Dessouki, "The Islamic Resurgence: Sources, Dynamics, and Implications," in *Islamic Resurgence in the Arab World*, (New York: Praeger Publishers, 1982), 16.

55. *Middle East Newsletter* 130 (Dec. 7, 1979–Jan.13, 1980): 7–8.

56. *Economist*, Dec. 13, 1980.

57. Dessouki, 13.

INTERNATIONAL LAW AFLOAT ON A SEA OF WORLD RELIGIONS

A FOCUS ON THE ROLE OF ISLAMIC RESURGENCE IN THE FOREIGN POLICY OF QADHDAFI

After the 1969 revolution where Qadhdafi came to power, a systematic program of institution *shari'a* was inaugurated. Qadhdafi's vision of the ideal Islamic state is the *Jamahiriya*, a state where Muslim masses rule themselves according to the *shari'a*. The particular tenets of his vision for the perfect theocratic Islamic society are articulated in his *Green Book*, the ideological treatise of his brand of Islam.[58]

The General Pattern of Erosion of Shari'a and Absorption of Western Legal Codes

An increasing phenomenon in Libya as well as the entire Arab world is the establishment of a Western-educated elite. This elite generally includes a large number lawyers and business professionals. As Mayer, professor at the Wharton School, remarks:

> Persons educated along European lines increasingly came to dominate legislative and judicial activities and, as lawyers, formed an influential, new professional class. So consistent was the progress of this Westernization of the law that it came to seem inexorable. Although Muslim clerics and other traditionally minded Muslims objected to the abandonment of the *shari'a* and even formed movements like the Muslim Brethren to campaign for its revival, the Westernized elites who ran the legal systems in Muslim countries remained indifferent to their concerns.[59]

There are two areas of law, however, not only in Libya but the whole Muslim world, that are so strongly imbedded in Libyan society that even the Western-influenced elite dare not

---

58. Ann Elizabeth Mayer, "Islamic Resurgence or New Prophethood: The Role of Islam in Qadhdafi's Ideology," in *Islamic Resurgence in the Arab World* (New York: Praeger Publishers, 1982), 196.

59. Mayer, 197.

touch—Qur'anic family and inheritance law.[60] According to the Qur'an, spouses own equal shares of marital property. The legal system prior to Qadhdafi's takeover was similar to the French model, and thus was similar to the system in Egypt, Syria, and Iraq. After Qadhdafi's successful revolution, a commission was established to examine current Libyan law and recommend steps to reform the legal system according to the *shari'a*. The most significant contribution of this commission was the reform of penal sanctions. The existing criminal code contrary to the *shari'a* was revoked and the five crimes in the Qur'an for which there is a criminal penalty, the *hadd*, were instituted. The criminal penalties include 100 lashes for fornication, 80 lashes for slanderous imputation of unchastity, 40 lashes for consumption of beverage alcohol, amputation of the hand for theft, and amputation of the hand and foot for brigandage. Minor changes to the then-existing legal system based on the *shari'a* was the provision for the state to collect part of the alms tax, the *zakat*.[61]

Qadhdafi's Role of Limiting the Shari'a in Libya

Qadhdafi's reforms, however, were not completely consistent with *shari'a*. First, Qadhdafi abolished separate jurisdiction of the *shari'a* courts, leaving all jurisdiction to secular courts. Second, the Islamic tradition of leaving a family *waqf*, a trust fund set up to provide designated beneficiaries with income, was also abolished. Third, the *shari'a* in domestic law was set aside by setting minimum ages for marriage, eliminating forced marriages, a reduction of an ex-husband's alimony if he could demonstrate the ex-wife was at fault, and allowing the wife the option of divorce if she could pay a court-determined indemnification to her husband.[62]

---

60. Ibid.
61. Muammar Qadhdafi, *The Green Book. Part One: The Solution of the Problem of Democracy* (London: Martin Brian and O'Keefe, 1976), 31.
62. Ibid., 198.

INTERNATIONAL LAW AFLOAT ON A SEA OF WORLD RELIGIONS

Qadhdafi's Redefinition of the Divine Law, the Shari'a

Qadhdafi's *Green Book* contains three parts. The first part, the *shari'at al-mujtama*, literally "law of society," outlines Qadhdafi's view of the basis of his new society. According to *shari'at* theory, Allah is the sole legislator who deposits his sacred law (*shari'a muqaddasa*) in the Qur'an and the *sunna*, or the customs of the Prophet Muhammad. Under classical *shari'a* theory, the *shari'a* exists in rigid form with no possibility for new legislation. The majority Sunni position is that the *shari'a* cannot be amended, altered, or modified. The *shari'a* exists solely to govern as it is, and the sole function of government is to provide a court implement whereby the *shari'a* can be applied. The *shiite* theory differs in that the *shiites* believe that divinely inspired imams in their religious capacities can make new laws.

Qadhdafi, therefore, in "good politician" style, claimed the rigid application of *shari'a* theory while at the same time excluded a major part of it. In part two of Qadhdafi's *Green Book*, Qadhdafi redefined the *shari'a* as containing solely the Qur'an, not the Sunna of the Prophet Muhammad and the vast corpus of commentary on the *shari'a* contained in the *fiqh*, the vast body of recorded medieval jurisprudence. In 1977, Libya adopted a new constitution establishing the authority of the Allah as sovereign and the people as subjects, but Allah's law as exposited by *Green Book*, and the people's rights and responsibilities as exposited by the *Green Book*.

Qadhdafi's Attack on Islamic Shirk or Para-Qur'anic Religious Documents

In one of Qadhdafi's speeches in 1978 he further articulated his unique doctrine of *shari'a*. He stated that the Prophet Muhammad was merely a vehicle for revelation according to Sura 46:9. Therefore, Muslims should look solely to the Qur'an for their religious authority rather than the Sunna of the Prophet. Further, Qadhdafi argued that the Qur'an, unlike the Bible, was accurately recorded.[63]

63. Muammar al-Qadhdafi, *al Sijill al-qawmi, bayanat wa kutab wa ahadith*

ORIENTATION

Qadhdafi assailed Christianity's Holy Book, contending the text of the Bible was not an accurate contemporaneous record, having been redacted by numerous later editors who merely recorded inflated hearsay that passed from generation to generation. According to Qadhdafi, mischievous compilers had adulterated the Bible with unsubstantiated alterations.[64] Faulty oral traditions incorporated into the Bible Qadhdafi called *shirk*. But Muslims should not follow *shirk*, either; because the Prophet's traditions were subject to *shirk* as much as the alleged oral traditions of the Christians.

In the same speech, Qadhdafi assailed the role of imams and clerics. Because the Qur'an was written in clear and understandable Arabic, no intermediary should come between the Qur'an and the Muslim. The Muslim should not regard imams as divine spokesmen. To Qadhdafi, the Qur'an alone is the mouthpiece of Allah. No one should ascend the *minbar*, the mosque's pulpit, to tell Muslims what they should believe. Islamic scholars were not an essential part of any Muslim's religion. Qadhdafi specifically attacked any para-Qur'anic writings as unnecessary to the full understanding of the Islamic faith. At a festival on July 3, 1978, at the largest mosque in Tripoli Qadhdafi preached the same doctrine of "sola Qur'an."[65] At the mosque the local cleric, the *ulama*, was in the congregation. The *ulama* and Qadhdafi argued over the validity of the *hadith*, the written reports about the Prophet's Muhammad's actions. Qadhdafi argued that the *hadith* was entirely unreliable historically and therefore no Muslim should hold the *hadith* as a source of religious authority. The *ulama* countered, holding that study of the *hadith* was a science that enabled the Muslim scholar to determine what

---

al-aqid Muaccmar al-Qadhdafi (Tripoli: Mathaat al-Thawra al-arabiy, 1978), 466–83 as cited by Mayer, 201.

64. Mayer, 201.

65. Qadhdafi here remarkably resembles the great Christian reformer, Martin Luther, in this doctrine. Luther held that although Christian scholars were helpful in determining the meaning of Scripture, they were not essential to understanding Scripture. On religious authority, Luther held the sole source of authority was the Bible, not the Church's clerics. To Luther, the issue in faith and practice was not "what does the church say the Scripture says?" but "what does the Scripture say?"

were reliable reports about the Prophet and what reports were not authentic. Although both Qadhdafi and the *ulama* agreed that there was a consensus, an *ijma*, that certain standard collections of the *hadith* were trustworthy, Qadhdafi nonetheless held that Muslims had no definite revelation from Allah or proof that false *hadith* had not been inserted into even these standard collections. Qadhdafi substantiated his claim by citing the historical milieu of the formulation of the *hadith*, where antecedents of the Sunni and Shiite branches of Islam fought over succession. Qadhdafi further substantiated his claim by citing self-contradictions in the *hadith* and between the *hadith* and the Qur'an.[66]

Qadhdafi's Standing with Shiite Revolutionaries

Although Qadhdafi was a fierce Arab nationalist, Shiites hardly regard him as persona grata. Qadhdafi's modification of the *shari'a*, his attacks on the *hadith*, his denials of the *ulama*, his denial of the authority of imams, clerics, and scholars caused the Shiite activists to cringe. To the Shiites, Qadhdafi was heterodox and should be either "instructed" or removed.[67] Qadhdafi had established his own unique Islamic theology where he alone became the preeminent prophet-lawgiver to the exclusion of any Muslim cleric. In the judicial sphere, Qadhdafi's own appointed secular judges composed the judiciary (the *shari'a* religious courts he abolished). In the political sphere, Qahdhafi's opponents had a marked predilection to disappearance. In the religious sphere, Qadhdafi's *Green Book* and the Qur'an were the sole written authoritative sources of Islamic religion.

---

66. Qadhdafi, 997–1009 as cited by Mayer 202.
67. Mayer, 218.

ORIENTATION

A FOCUS ON THE IRANIAN REVOLUTION AND ITS DOCTRINE OF INTERNATIONAL EXPANSION

Islam as a Catalyst for International Revolution

The Ayatollah Khomeini was not trained as a politician, neither as a diplomat but rather as a theological teacher. Because of his fierce attacks on monarchy, he was exiled by the Shah of Iran. Khomeini, however, made great use of annual pilgrimages to Mecca. At such festivals, he decried monarchy as a form of government that was anti-Qur'anic and condemned Iran becoming an American vassal state. In 1977, the Democratic Presidential candidate, Jimmy Carter, called for a better human-rights record from America's allies. His call spurred the Shah to release over three hundred political prisoners. These prisoners included some of the Islamic intelligentsia—lawyers, politicians, and Islamic clerics. More and more, at the orchestration of Khomeini, various sectors of society took to the streets in demonstrations. Khomeini, who himself was Shiite, addressed the Iranian military, which was largely Shiite. He told the Iranian war machine that those who shoot at their fellow Muslims are shooting at the Qur'an. With the overthrow of the Shah, Khomeini returned to a national assembly of 2 million at Tehran who demanded an Islamic state. Later, a national referendum consisted of a single question: "Should Iran become an Islamic Republic?" Every Iranian had an identity card that would be stamped "yes" should they vote yes. Therefore, out of fear of being labeled an infidel, over 89 percent of the populace voted in the national referendum. Of those who voted, over 90 percent voted "yes," thus having their identity cards stamped "yes." At that point, Khomeini declared the beginning of the "Government of Allah."[68]

The mosque had become the vestibule of a new religious order in Iran. At the mosques Khomeini had established revolutionary committees to orchestrate the revolution in Iran. Khomeini's Friday sermons at the *minbar* became the chief inspiration for revolt.

---

68. Dilip Hiro, *Holy Wars: The Rise of Islamic Fundamentalism* (New York: Routledge, 1989), 164–69.

International revolution against monarchy and the establishment of Islamic republics became the religious international call. Therefore, the Shia branch of Islam became a synonym for international religious revolution. Shia was infused with a new militancy by *imams* such as Khomeini who were deemed to be new inspired prophets of Allah to lead the *Dar al Islam*, the Realm of Islam, from the darkness of infidelity to national Qur'anic observance.

The International Ramifications of the Rise of Ayatollah Khomeini

The rise of the Ayatollah Khomeini's institution of *Valiat-Faghih* in Iran illustrates an implementation of Islamic theocracy.[69] The domestic structure of the Iranian theocracy also reflects the theocratic principle. Under Article 91, a council of twelve individuals appointed by the "maximum leader," the Ayatollah, oversees the Iranian Parliament to confirm that each of its resolutions is consistent with Islamic principles. Six of the council are Muslim clerics appointed by the *Valiat-Faghih*. The other six are Muslim lawyers chosen by the Parliament. Under Article 93, the Parliament's authority is null and void without the sanction of the council of twelve. In event of deadlock in the council of twelve, the supremacy of the clerics is established by Article 96. Article 3 (16) of the Iranian constitution articulates the foreign policy of Iran. All foreign relations must be "based on Islamic principles, brotherly commitment towards all Muslims and the complete support for the oppressed peoples of the world."[70] Therefore, the interstate relations of the Iranian theocracy are merely an extension of the theocratic principle.

---

69. Reisman, p. 118; Ayatollah Ruhollah Khomeini, *Islamic Government* (Arlington, V.A.: Joint Publications Research Service, 1979), 105.

70. Reisman, 121.

ORIENTATION

Militant Shia Fueling War with Iraq

With Khomeini's grip on power firm in Iran, he began to denounce secularists such as the Baathist Party in Iraq, including the Baathist president Hussein. Hussein, from the outset of the Iranian Revolution, had been receiving reports of low morale in the Iranian military and general societal undercurrents decrying the new religious despotism. With non-Shiites populating the oil-rich province on the Iraq-Iran border, Hussein ordered his forces to "liberate" this province. The Iraqi forces however were stalemated.

But the Iraqi attack caused the Iranian Islamic revolution to move from its anti-American phase, as evidenced by the taking of the American embassy and its hostages, into a patently antisecularized Arab phase. Khomeini, from the early days in the war with Iraq, denounced Saddam Hussein as a "pagan." Khomeini stated that since Hussein had attacked the Iranian Islamic Republic after its self-declaration as a "Government of Allah," Hussein had actually attacked Allah and those who serve him according to the Qur'an. Therefore, true Muslims should see the war with Iraq as a *jihad*, or holy war with infidels.[71]

National Statutes Resulting from the Shiite Revolution

The Shiite Revolution in Iran established a new order predicated on various Articles drafted by the Islamic Parliament. Those who drafted the constitution conceded to demands of the primarily Sunni Kurds, Baluchs, and Arabs for tolerance of Islamic sects other than Shiite. Article 12 of the Iranian constitution states:

> The official religion of Iran is Islam and the Twelver Jaafari school of thought, and this principle shall remain eternally immutable. Other Islamic schools of thought, including the Hanafi, Shafii, Maliki, Hanbali, and Zaidi schools, are to be accorded full respect, and their followers are free to act in accordance with their own

---

71. Dilip Hiro, *Holy Wars: The Rise of Islamic Fundamentalism* (New York: Routledge, 1989), 180–84.

jurisprudence in performing their religious devotions. These schools enjoy official status for the purpose of religious education and matters of personal status (marriage, divorce, inheritance and bequests), being accepted in the courts relating to such matters.

Article 5 of the constitution states because of the death of Hazrat Vali Asr or Lord of the Age, the missing Twelfth Imam,

> The governance and leadership of the nation devolve upon the just and pious *faqih* who is acquainted with the circumstances of his age; courageous, resourceful and possessed of administrative ability; and recognized and accepted as Leader by the majority of the people.[72]

The replacement of the twelfth imam is described in Article 1 as the "Grand Ayatollah Imam Khomeini." A replacement for the Ayatollah will be according to Article 107:

> Whenever a candidate who has outstanding characteristics for leadership is found, he will be introduced to the people as the Leader. Otherwise, three or five candidates who fulfill the conditions for leadership will be appointed members of the Leadership Council and introduced to the people.[73]

The leader must be fully conversant with "the issues of the day and circumstances of his age."[74]

Although the constitution outlines the place for a "maximum leader," the first chapter of the constitution describes the application of the basic Qur'anic principle of community. Chapter one establishes a multitiered system of government. The multitiered system issues from the Qur'anic texts 42:38, "their affairs are by consultation among them," and 3:153, "consult them on affairs." The Iranian constitution lays out three branches, executive, legislative, and judicial. The judicial branch, according to a descending

---

72. Hiro, 172–73.

73. Dilip Hiro, *Holy Wars: The Rise of Islamic Fundamentalism* (New York: Routledge, 1989), 173.

74. Hiro, 175.

order of appellate relation, includes Supreme Judicial Council, a Provincial Council, Municipal Council, and City, Neighborhood, Division, Village Council.

The rights of the citizens of the Islamic Republic of Iran are delineated by the new constitution. The judiciary, according to Article 156, has the function of "restoring public rights and promoting justice and legitimate freedoms."[75] Chapter Three of the constitution contains twenty-three articles. Article 21 includes the rights of women according to "Islamic criteria." Article 24 states what are the rights of the press: "Publications and the press are free to present all matters except those that are detrimental to the fundamentals of Islam or the rights of the public." Article 26 also states the right to political parties: "the formation of political and professional parties, associations and societies, as well as religious societies, whether they be Islamic or pertain to one of the recognized religious communities is freely permitted on the condition that they do not violate the principles of independence, freedom, national unity, the criteria of Islam or the basis of the Islamic Republic." Article 26 goes further to state: "No one may be prevented from participating in the above groups, or be compelled to participate in them."[76]

Article 49 delineates the right to property, subject to government limitations:

> The government has the responsibility of confiscating all wealth resulting from usury, usurpation, bribery, embezzlement, theft, gambling, misuse of endowments, misuse of government contracts and transactions, the sale of uncultivated lands and other categories of land inherently subject to public ownership, the operations of houses of ill-repute, and other illegal sources.[77]

Article 49 further outlines the property rights under the Iranian Republic:

---

75. Ibid.
76. Hiro, 176–77.
77. Hiro, 176.

> When appropriate, such wealth must be restored to its legitimate owner, and if no such owner can be identified it must be placed in the public treasury. The application of this principle must be accompanied by investigation and verification in accordance with the law of Islam and carried out by the government.[78]

Article 35 describes the jurisprudential rights of the citizen of the Islamic Republic. In any dispute, "both parties to a dispute have the right in all courts of law to select a lawyer." Article 35 states "if they are unable to do so, arrangements must be made to provide them with legal counsel."[79] Further, Article 38 forbids the use of torture, and adds that the punishment of those who violate the ban "will be determined by law." Article 25 provides for privacy rights for Iranian citizens. The following is forbidden:

> Inspections of letters and the failure to deliver them, the recording and disclosure of telephone conversations, the disclosure of telegraphic and telex communications, or the willful failure to deliver them, wiretapping and all forms of covert investigation.[80]

Although the rights delineated may please the Western ear, reports continue to pour in from Iran regarding the torture of prisoners.

THE IMPACT OF THE CONSTITUTION OF THE ISLAMIC REPUBLIC UPON INTERNATIONAL LAW

The Pan-Islamic Component of the Iranian Constitution

The Iranian Constitution is definitively pan-Islamic according to Article 10: "This your nation is a single nation." As Article 10 states:

---

78. Ibid.

79. Dilip Hiro, *Holy Wars: The Rise of Islamic Fundamentalism* (New York: Routledge, 1989), 176.

80. Hiro, 176.

> The government of the Islamic Republic of Iran has the duty of formulating its general policies with a view to the merging and union of all Muslim peoples, and it must constantly strive to bring about political, economic and cultural unity of the Islamic world.[81]

Article 152 is more specific, stating that the Islamic Republic's foreign policy includes the "defense of the rights of all Muslims" and the "non-alignment with respect to the hegemonist superpowers."[82] Article 154 "sanctifies" the export of revolution as the religious duty of Iranian citizens:

> The Islamic Republic of Iran considers the attainment of independence, freedom and just government to be the right of all peoples in the world. It therefore protects the just struggles of the oppressed and deprived in every corner of the globe.

Khomeini declared that the "Islamic duty" of its citizens was to support national liberation movements of the "deprived peoples" of the world. Khomeini's foreign minister, Ibrahim Yazdi, stated regarding oppressed peoples in 1979 that the Khomeini regime "only wanted [them] to benefit from Iran's experience and gain strength from Iran's support."[83] Khomeini states that "if the revolution kept within Iranian borders, it would become vulnerable."[84]

Therefore, the export of Shiite revolution is not only desirable to the new Iranian regime, it is part and parcel of their domestic law. Religion and state eclipse in the Iranian constitution, causing both law and religion to serve the single end of converting all of Islam, and later the entire world to the republican form of Shiite government, i.e., the "government of Allah." The establishment of a worldwide fellowship of Islamic republics is the end of the Iranian constitution.

---

81. Hiro, 207.
82. Hiro, 207.
83. Hiro, 207–8.
84. Dilip Hiro, *Holy Wars: The Rise of Islamic Fundamentalism* (New York: Routledge, 1989), 208.

INTERNATIONAL RESPONSE TO THE IRANIAN REVOLUTION

The Formation of the Gulf Cooperation Council

The open statements of the Iranian constitution regarding the export, including armed export, of Shiite revolution caused the various surrounding Arab states, especially those with large populations of Shiites, to fear for their present existence. Since the Iranian revolution claims to be republican, the democratic aura of the Iranian revolution may appeal to the politically voiceless masses of the various modern feudal monarchies—Kuwait, Saudi Arabia, Qatar, the United Arab Emirates, and Oman. Because of fear of internal disorder, if not outright revolt, Kuwait, Saudi Arabia, Qatar, the United Arab Emirates, and Oman formed the Gulf Cooperation Council. This supranational body would even call upon the help of the West "for military assistance in case of serious threat to one or more of its members."[85] The goals of the Gulf Cooperation Council are to "co-ordinate internal security, procurement of arms and the national economies of the six member states."[86]

Specific responses of the member nations to the Iranian revolution have been fierce. The Bahraini prime minister stated, for instance, "The Iranian regime is instigating the Shias in Bahrain and the Gulf under the slogans of the Islamic revolution . . . training them in the use of weapons and acts of sabotage and sending them to their countries to foment chaos and destroy security."[87] The Saudi interior minister, Prince Nayif, offered to send Saudi troops to Bahrain to help prevent a coup. According to Nayif, "the sabotage plot was engineered by the Iranian government and was directed against Saudi Arabia." As a result of Iranian expansionism, the Gulf leaders have drawn together to maintain their

---

85. Hiro, 210.
86. Hiro, 210.
87. Hiro, 211.

authoritative regimes. They will not let loose of their monopoly on political power easily.[88]

The militant Shiite vision of a "government of Allah" over all nations will not be realized without massive bloodshed even among the other conservative Arab states. The union of the Arab world around Shiite revolutionary goals will not occur with just the dire opposite of the peaceful harmony the Qur'anic concept of *umma* requires. Worldwide international Islamic utopia appears a great way off.

---

88. Hiro, 211.

THE ISSUE OF KUWAITI CONSTITUTIONAL INTEGRITY

The Kuwaiti Constitution Purports to Guarantee "Absolute" Freedom of Religion

DISTINGUISHING REAL LAW FROM "WINDOW DRESSING"

As a force of law, the Kuwaiti Constitution is problematic because of dubious phraseology, implied subordination to Islamic law, and implied subordination to the ruling Amir.

Dubious Phraseology

"Law," as a governing entity, is dubious in various Articles—national symbols are "specified by law" (Article 5), "property, capital, and work" are "individual rights" "regulated by law" (Article 18), confiscation of property is "specified by law" (Article 19), employment relations are "regulated by law" (Article 22), alien patriation is "specified by law" (Article 26), "liberty of movement" is "in accordance with provisions of law" (Article 31), "the right to express and propagate" opinion is "in accordance with the conditions and procedures specified by law" (Article 36), "freedom of the press" is "in accordance with the conditions and procedures specified by law" (Article 37), entrance to places of residence is only "in the circumstances and manner specified by law" (Article 38), "freedom of communication" is not censored "except in the circumstances and manner specified by law" (Article 39), education is "in accordance with law" (Article 40), "forced labor" is prohibited "except in the cases specified by law" (Article 42), "private assembly" is permitted "in accordance with the conditions and manner specified by law" (Article 44), "military service" is "regulated by law" (Article 47), the Amir may "decree, issue sanctions and regulations necessary for the organization of public services and administration, not conflicting with any law" (Article 73), taxation is "by a law" (Article 134), "public loans" are concluded "by a law" (Article 136) as are other financial matters, calendar (Article 139), budget (Articles 140, 144), and appropriation (Article 142).[1]

Law, however, in its formation and enforcement is insufficiently defined. In the discussion of separation of powers, the Amir becomes the architect of all legislative, executive, and judicial power.

Functional Constitutional Subordination to Islamic Law

Shari'a as "a Main Source" of Law

The Kuwaiti Constitution's Article 2, "the religion of the State is Islam, and the Islamic Shari'a shall be a main source of legislation," implies totalitarian religious uniformity, regardless of whether Shari'a is "a" or "the" main source[2] of law.[3] Although the Kuwaiti National Assembly voted 39–11 to maintain Article 2's phraseology of "a main source of legislation," the distinction is tantamount

---

1. Kuwait Constitution, translated in Albert Blaustein & Gilbert H. Flanz, *Constitutions of the Countries of the World: Kuwait* (1991), 12

2. Kuwait Constitution, translated in Albert Blaustein & Gilbert H. Flanz, *Constitutions of the Countries of the World: Kuwait* (1991), 12

3. "Human beings do not ever make laws; it is the accidents and catastrophes of all kinds happening in every conceivable way, that make laws for us." Plato, Laws IV 709; Sarah Rumage, "The Return of Article 42: Enemy of the Good for Collective Security," 5 *Pace Intl L. Rev.* (1993): 211, 286.

to no difference. If shari'a is a main source, this source, by definition, obviates contradictory sources because shari'a claims absolute precedence.

Shari'a includes four components: the Qur'an, which has only 600 lines of defined legal stipulations,[4] the Hadith, statements and deeds of Muhammed and the Imams (Imams are the rightful successors to the Prophet in the Shiite branch of Islam),[5] the "ijma," the consensus of Islamic legal scholars[6] and the "aqi," the sitting judges' analogic reasoning in adjudicating cases.[7]

Qur'anic Basis for Statecraft

In the first component of shari'a, a variety of Qur'anic passages constitutes fundaments of Islamic political theory. These passages guide traditional Islamic statecraft:

> Sura 3:26: "Say: O Allah! Owner of the Kingdom! Thou givest kingdom to whom Thou wilt and takest it away from whom Thou wilt."
>
> Sura 4:65: "Nay, O Muhammad! by thy Lord, they will not be believers until they accept you as the final arbiter in all their disputes and submit to your decision wholeheartedly without any heartache."
>
> Sura 7:3: "Follow the revelation sent unto you from your Lord and do not follow the (so called) guardians other than Him."
>
> Sura 7:54: "Beware! His is the creation and His is the (right to) Rule."

---

4. Michael M.J. Fischer, "Legal Postulates in Flux: Justice, Wit, and Hierarchy in Iran," in *Law and Islam in the Middle East* (Daisy Hilse Dwyer, ed., 1990), 115–17.

5. Nader Entessar, "Criminal Law and the Legal System in Revolutionary Iran," 8 *B.C. Third World L.J.* (1988): 91–92.

6. Entessar; Fischer, 121.

7. Entessar; Fischer, 121.

THE ISSUE OF KUWAITI CONSTITUTIONAL INTEGRITY

Sura 12:40: "The (right of) Command is for none but Allah. he hath commanded that ye follow none but Him. That is the right way (of life)."

Sura 13:111: "None is a partner in His Sovereignty."

Sura 114:1–3: "Say (O Muhammad): I seek refuge in the Sustainer of mankind, the Sovereign (Ruler) of mankind, the Lord of mankind."[8]

These passages presuppose a monism of organized religion and state, demanding the exclusivity of Islam as a source of substantive law and practical adjudication.

The Purpose of the Islamic State

The first objective of the Islamic state, according Sohail Mahmood, is "to make Shariah the law of the land."[9] In the late 1970s, for instance, Kuwait, along with Egypt and the United Arab Emirates, established review bodies assigned to revise law according to the Islamic shari'a. In the early 1970s Libya, in 1977–78, Pakistan, post-revolution Iran, in 1983–85 and after 1989, Sudan went further by instituting Islamization—institution of the shari'a—as "central official policy."[10] Kurdi states the purpose of the Islamic

---

8. See generally Sayyid Abul a'la Maududi, *The Islamic Law and Constitution* (1990), 253–72 (articulating the Shi'a theory of Islamic statecraft).

9. See generally Sohail Mahmood, *The Concept of an Islamic State* (1989), 28 (arguing, according to "Khomeiniite" Shi'a theory, for the replacement of "decadent monarchy rule with some sort of democratic republics").

10. See Ann Elizabeth Mayer, "Religious Law and Legal Pluralism: Islam and the State," 12 *Cardozo L. Rev.* (February/March 1991): 1015, 1029; see also, Esposito, Sudan, *The Politics of Islamic Revivalism* (S. Hunter ed. 1988), 187–203; see A. Iqbal, *Islamisation of Pakistan* (1986), 107–37; see "Comment, Islamic Law and Modern Government: Saudi Arabia Supplements the Shari'a to Regulate Development," 18 *Colum. J. Transat'l L.* (1980): 413; see generally, *Islam in the Political Process* (J. Piscator ed. 1983); see Interview with King Fahd, King of Saudi Arabia, in Kuwait (March 28, 1992), quoted in "Empty Reforms, Saudi Arabia's New Basic Laws," *Middle East Watch* (May 1992): 2; see Amnesty International, "Saudi Arabia: Religious Intolerance: The Arrest, Detention and Torture of Christian Worshippers and Shi'a Muslims" (1993); see Nadjm Oud-Dine Bammate, "Freedom According to Islam," in *Christianity*

state in universalistic terms, but qualifies the concern of the Islamic is "primarily" for Muslims only:

> The primary purposes of the Islamic State are the ensurance of freedom from outside invasions, the security of domestic tranquillity and the provision of justice, equality and personal security for its people. . . . Of course, the application of the Islamic Holy Constitution, the promotion of individual interests and the general welfare of Muslims are among the primary and significant issues with which the Islamic State has to deal.[11]

If the Christian minority are to have any place in the Islamic state, according to Islamic clerics Mawdudi and Qutb, the minority must be made to "feel the strength of Islam, its grandeur and supremacy, [as well as] its goodness, generosity and tolerance; that is a state that would push them—on the whole to enter Islam."[12] The more extreme fundamentalist elements in both the Sunni and Shi'a camps throughout the Arab world decry the "secular"

---

and Freedom: A Symposium (1955), 34–50; see Karima Bennoune, "As-Salamu Alaykum? Humanitarian Law in Islamic Jurisprudence," *Mich.J. Int'l L.* 15 (1994): 605; see A.K. Brohi, "The Nature of Islamic Law and the Concept of Human Rights in Islam, 41.60 *Kuwait: International Commission of Jurists* (1980); see Donna E. Arzt, "Religious Human Rights in the World Today: A Report on the 1994 Atlanta Conference with Book Excerpts, Religious Human Rights in Muslim States of the Middle East and North Africa," 10 *Emory Int'l. Rev.* (Spring 1996): 139; see John Makdisi and Marianne Makdisi, "Islamic Law Bibliography: Revised and Updated List of Secondary Sources," 87 *Law Libr. J.* (Winter 1995): 69.

11. See generally Abdulrahman Abdulkadir Kurdi, *The Islamic State: A Study Based on the Islamic Holy Constitution* (1984), 64 (outlining an Islamic religious constitutional theory). See generally, Mehdi Mozaffari, *Authority in Islam: From Mumammad to Khomeini* (1987), 47–91 (delineating categories of the monoliths of authority in Islamic states, including monist models, where clerics control the state (e.g. Iran), semi-monist models, where power is shared by politicians and clerics (e.g. Algeria and the Ba'th states, Syria and Iraq), dualist models, where power is divided into spheres, the clerical and the legal (e.g. Saudi Arabia), and fusionist models, where the political leader assumes clerical leadership (e.g. Libya)).

12. See Nazih N. Ayubi, *Political Islam: Religion and Politics in the Arab World* (1991), 145.

Egyptian constitution because it equates Muslims with non-Muslims.[13] Ideological totalitarianism is the goal of Shi'a revolutionaries. Islamic ideological conformity is the objective of revolutionary Shi'a—"a time it will become impossible in the changed society . . . for any other system of life to maintain its existence."[14]

If shari'a is "a main source" of legislation, it must, by definition, be the supreme law of the land because shari'a forbids any law contrary to itself. As Masudul Hasan argues: "unless there is a specific provision in the Constitution recognizing the Shariah as the fundamental law the judicial system cannot be Islamic."[15] The conservative elements in both Sunni and Shi'a camps argue that Islam must necessarily control the state: "It cannot be said that Islam is established unless it takes the form of a State."[16] Ideological uniformity, therefore, in all realms is, by definition, the objective of shari'a.

Subordination to the Ruling Amir

The Amir, more than the Kuwaiti Constitution, is the functional law in Kuwait.[17] Article 4 acknowledges Kuwait is ruled by a he-

13. Ibid.

14. Sayyed Abulala Maudoodi, *The Process of Islamic Revolution* (1955) (outlining the pattern of Islamic revolutionary takeover of a society by first discipling Islamic ideologues in every sector of society, then establishment of Islam by force of law).

15. Masudul Hasan, *Reconstruction of Political Thought in Islam* (1988), 209. See generally Muhammad Hadi Hussain and Abdul Hameed Kamali, *The Nature of the Islamic State* (1977) (tracing political developments in the world of Islam, including the legitimization of accession to power by force, according to the precedent set by Mu'awiya in A.D. 661, after the first four essentially democratic caliphates).

16. Nazih N. Ayubi, *Political Islam: Religion and Politics in the Arab World* (1991), 145.

17. International Court of Justice, "Judgment on Jurisdiction and Admissibility in the Case concerning Maritime Delimitation and Territorial Questions Between Qatar and Bahrain (Qatar v. Bahrain)," 34 *I.L.M.*: 1204 1226 (demonstrating the authoritarian regimes of Qatar and Bahrain, effecting unfettered control over "Rump Parliament" and the courts).

reditary ruling caste, with an "heir apparent" and his designated descendants, contra Article 6, establishing a "democratic" system of government, "under which sovereignty resides in the people, the sources of all powers." Article 50 claims "separation of powers,"[18] but Articles 51, 52, and 53 place all legislative and executive power in the Amir and judicial power in the courts, who exercise power "in the name of the Amir."[19] "The name of" signifies authority derived from the Amir. As Robert Allen Dahl argues in *Preface to Democratic Theory*, prevailing cultural and social values rule the populace more than any piece of paper. Constitutions do not make republics or constitutional monarchies; the prevailing cultural and social values of the people do.[20] The tribalistic sociology renders

18. Separation of powers prevents tyranny because it provides an external check upon the tyrannical impulses of officials. Separation of powers provides an external check because it guarantees that the ambitions of individual in one branch will counteract those in another. Countermanding ambitions will be effective because the individuals in one branch can invoke the threat of rewards and punishments against tyrannical individuals in the other branch or branches. Dahl at 20. Further, the Constitution prevents the legislature from tyrannizing the minority. As Hamilton posited: "No legislative act, contrary to the Constitution, can be valid. To deny this would be to affirm that the deputy is greater than his principal; that the servant is above the master; that the representatives of the people are superior to the people themselves; that men acting by virtue of powers may do not only what their powers forbid." *Federalist Papers*, No. 78, p. 467. Hamilton, therefore, envisioned Constitutional law as a permanent check upon tyranny, whether tyranny of the many, tyranny of the few, or the tyranny of one.

19. Kuwait Constitution, translated in 10 Albert Blaustein & Gilbert H. Flanz, *Constitutions of the Countries of the World: Kuwait* (1991), 12.

20. As an empirical generalization, Madison understood that the accumulation of all powers, legislative, executive, and judiciary in the same hands implies the elimination of external checks. The elimination of external checks produces tyranny. Therefore the accumulation of all powers in the same hands implies tyranny. *The Federalist*, ed. Edward Mead Earle ("The Modern Library" New York: Random House, n. d.), 313. Moreover, if unrestrained by external checks, a minority of individuals will tyrannize over a majority of individuals. Dahl's rendition of Madison as per *The Debates in the Several State Conventions on the Adoption of the Federal Constitution as Recommended by the General Convention at Philadelphia*, in 1787, *Together with the Journal of Federal Convention*, etc., ed. Jonathan Elliot (2d ed.; Phil.: Lippincott, 1941), V, 203. Conversely, if unrestrained by external checks, a majority of individuals will

THE ISSUE OF KUWAITI CONSTITUTIONAL INTEGRITY

the Kuwaiti Constitution little more than window dressing for the community of nations.

Real Hope for Peaceful Change Lies in the Amir

The central federal power to curb human rights abuse in Kuwait is currently the Amir's.[21] The peaceful establishment of the rule of law in Kuwait necessitates the Amir's self-subordination—that is, the evolution of an absolute monarchy to a constitutional monarchy. Not unlike the development in the United Kingdom of an unwritten constitution which governs and limits the ruling dynasty, the

---

tyrannize over a minority of individuals.

As Hamilton expressed the principle succinctly, "Give all power to the many, they will oppress the few. Give all power to the few, they will oppress the many." *The Debates in the Several State Conventions on the Adoption of the Federal Constitution as Recommended by the General Convention at Philadelphia, in 1787, Together with the Journal of Federal Convention,* etc., ed. Jonathan Elliot (2d ed.; Phil.: Lippincott, 1941), V, 203. Madison's understanding of a representative democracy, a republic, was a governmental system which derives all of its powers directly or indirectly from the great body of the people and is administered by persons holding their office during their pleasure, for a limited period, or during good behavior. The Federalist, No. 39.

21. See Carlyle Murphy, "Kuwait Reported Moving to Curb Rights Abuses," *Washington Post*, October 2, 1991, A30. Compare Human Rights Watch, "Punishing the Victim: Rape and Mistreatment of Asian Maids in Kuwait" (1992).

Amir's prioritization of the power of law above his own[22] would herald his virtue to the international community.[23]

DISTINGUISHING THE KUWAITI CONSTITUTION FROM CONDUCT, "PAPER" FROM PRACTICE

Despite the putative claims of the Kuwaiti Constitution ensuring fundamental rights, the U.S. State Department has correctly inveighed against the Kuwaiti Sheikhdom before the Iraqi invasion for "its feudalistic and unrepresentative structure" effecting gross abuse of human rights.[24]

---

22. A variety of delegates to the American Constitutional convention perceived basic human nature as a ravenous power monger. Lenoir, in the North Carolina debates, warned that "we ought to consider the depravity of human nature, the predominant thirst of power which is in the breast of everyone, the temptations rulers may have." *The Debates in the Several State Conventions on the Adoption of the Federal Constitution as Recommended by the General Convention at Philadelphia, in 1787. Together with the Journal of Federal Convention*, etc., ed. Jonathan Elliot (2d ed.; Philadelphia: Lippincott, 1941), IV, 204. Franklin, at the Federal Convention, joined the chorus: "There are two passions which have a powerful influence on the affairs of men. These are ambition and avarice; the love of power and the love of money." V, 145. Hamilton, at the Federal Convention, agreed that "men love power." V, 200. Mason articulated the same perspective at the Federal Convention: "From the nature of man, we may be sure that those who have power in their hands . . . will always, when they can . . . increase it." V, 294.

Jefferson said "one hundred and seventy three despots would surely be as oppressive as one . . . an elective despotism was not the government we fought for." *The Federalist*, No. 48, 324. Not forgetting ample historical examples of despotism, the American founding fathers concluded human nature was inherently dangerous because of an inherent lust for power.

23. Compare 1 Samuel 8:7-18, 12:17; Sarvenaz Bahar, "Khomeinism, The Islamic Republic of Iran, and International Law: The Relevance of Islamic Political Theology," 33 *Harvard Int'l L.J.* (1992):145 (explaining Khomeini's anti-monarchical appeals and espousals of democratic theory as calling cards of the Iranian revolution).

24. See "Country Reports on Human Rights Practices for 1990: Report Submitted to the Committee on Foreign Relations, U.S. Senate, and the Committee on Foreign Affairs, House of Representatives, by the Department of State" (February 1991), 1507-21. See also "Country Reports on Human Rights Practices for 1991: Report Submitted to the Committee on Foreign Relations,

THE ISSUE OF KUWAITI CONSTITUTIONAL INTEGRITY

Feudalistic and Unrepresentative Power Structure

Specifically, the Sheikdom denies its citizens the right of assembly and the right to "change their government" by peaceful means.[25] The Amir, "always . . . a descendent of the al-Sabah family," exercises unfettered authority, without checks and balances, as evidenced by his unilaterally dissolving the National Assembly and ruling by imperial decree.[26] By decree, prominent Kuwaiti opposition[27] leaders suffered "physical violence" in apprehension and interrogation.[28] The Amir charged the opposition leaders with "unlicensed activities"[29] because political parties were banned. "Vocal opposition" to the Sheikhdom resulted in arrest.[30]

Gross Human Rights Abuses

Human rights abuses included "arbitrary arrest, mistreatment of prisoners, and lack of due process in its trials."[31] The press censored,[32] "political and civil rights of all Kuwaiti residents"[33] restricted, and torture not uncommon,[34] the pre-invasion Kuwaiti human rights record is disturbing.[35]

U.S. Senate, and the Committee on Foreign Affairs, House of Representatives, by the Department of State" (February 1992); Shaw J. Dallai, "International Law and the United Nations' Role in the Gulf Crisis," 18 *Syracuse J. Int'l & Com.* (1992): 111, 140.

25. "Country Reports on Human Rights Practices for 1990," 1509–11, 1516–17; Dallai, 111, 129 (1992).

26. "Country Reports on Human Rights Practices for 1990," 1507

27. "Country Reports on Human Rights Practices for 1990," 1510.

28. "Country Reports on Human Rights Practices for 1990," 1509.

29. "Country Reports on Human Rights Practices for 1990," 1510.

30. "Country Reports on Human Rights Practices for 1990," 1513.

31. "Country Reports on Human Rights Practices for 1990, 1507.

32. "Country Reports on Human Rights Practices for 1990," 1507.

33. "Country Reports on Human Rights Practices for 1990, 1507.

34. "Country Reports on Human Rights Practices for 1990," 1509.

35. See generally Shaw J. Dallai, "International Law and the United Nations' Role in the Gulf Crisis," 18 *Syracuse J. Int'l & Com.* (1992): 111.

INTERNATIONAL LAW AFLOAT ON A SEA OF WORLD RELIGIONS

THE ANALYSIS OF ARTICLE 35, "FREEDOM OF RELIGION IS ABSOLUTE," IN THE KUWAITI CONSTITUTION—DOES THE ARTICLE HAVE TEETH?

Historical Origins

The Drafting of Kuwaiti Constitution

After the Treaty of Independence in 1961, the Amir of Kuwait, desiring the new nation's recognition in the world family of nations, applied and acquired U.N. membership. Further, to establish national credibility, and downplay the feudal monarchical power structure, the Amir instigated a constitutional convention. The Amir announced a provisional government during the convention's convening. On November 11, 1962, the Amir approved the constitution without alteration. On January 23, 1963, Kuwait held its first election, the country having been divided into ten voting districts, each allotted five seats. For the fifty seats, 210 candidates competed, although political party formation and affiliation was illegal. Some views binding the various candidates however included pan-Arab unity, more rapid constitutional and democratic reforms, and conservative enforcement of Islamic custom.[36]

Significantly, however, the heads of all ministries are appointed by the Amir. The ministers may respond to inquiries from committees composed of Assembly members. Further, the prime minister, who presides over the Assembly, is appointed by the Amir. But ultimately, the Assembly is tantamount to an advisory body—the Amir can dissolve it at will, as he did in 1976. Essentially, if the Amir wants advice, he will ask for it from the Assembly. If does not want the advice, he will let the Assembly offer it anyway. If he disagrees with the advice, he may ignore it. If he seriously

---

36. Ministry of Guidance and Information on Kuwait, "Modern Kuwait: A Welfare State (n.d.), 52–53; compare Abdalla S. Bujra, *The Politics of Stratification: A Study of Political Change in a South Arabian Town* (1971), 164–96 (outlining polarization into political camps, leading to beginnings of political parties).

objects to the advice, he can perform an Islamic "Pride's purge," and eliminate counter-elites or critics, and shape an Islamic Rump Parliament. Or, he can dissolve the entire Assembly, and, at his sole discretion, call for a new election, according to the precedent set in 1976.[37]

Examples of Constitutional Evolution in the Islamic World

Before the Twentieth Century

A variety of Muslim historians look to the Constitution of Medina in the early seventh century as the first functioning written body of political law in the world of Islam. The Constitution of Medina in the time of Muhammad (ca. 622) altered the direction of prayer from Jerusalem to Mecca.[38] After Muhammad, the first four caliphates were democratically chosen by vote of local rulers, and rule by consensus was the norm. A.D. 661, however, witnessed the legitimation of accession of power by force, according to the precedent set by the Caliph Mu'awiya.[39] For the next centuries, caliphs in the Arab, Seljuk Turkish, and Ottoman Turkish empires ascended according to rule of the jungle, the most powerful contender generally able to take the throne. The Ottoman Empire, however, comparing itself against liberalization of Western powers, developed its own constitution in 1876. But the Ottoman Constitution of 1876 did little to limit the monarch to create a "constitutional Caliphate." This constitution, not unlike Kuwait's, essentially vested all authority in the Caliphate.[40]

---

37. See generally Jill Crystal, *Kuwait: The Transformation of an Oil State* (1992), 3-27; h.r.p. Dickson, *Kuwait and Her Neighbors* (1956) (chronicling the history of Kuwait before the constitution); David Sapsted, *Modern Kuwait* (1980), 77-86; Croom Helm, *Mmeri Report: Kuwait* (1985), 15-52.

38. Kemal A. Faruki, *The Evolution of Islamic Constitutional Theory and Practice from 610 to 1926* (1971), 13-15.

39. Muhammad Hadi Hussain and Abdul Hameed Kamali, *The Nature of the Islamic State* (1977).

40. Kemal A. Faruki, *The Evolution of Islamic Constitutional Theory and Practice from 610 to 1926* (1971), 147.

INTERNATIONAL LAW AFLOAT ON A SEA OF WORLD RELIGIONS

Twentieth-Century Examples of Constitutional Evolution in the Islamic World

The Iranian Constitution of 1906 was not secular, separating organized religion from the state. Rather, the monarch was to be a follower of the Jafari law school of Twelver Shi'ism and defender of the faith. Parliament was to include five eminent clerics to filter any legislation contrary to Islamic law. The monarch was to be accountable to the representative assembly. The Pahlavi dynasty largely ignored the constitution, however, instituting Western dress codes, equating loyalty to the ruling family with Iranian nationalism, and coercing the clerics rather than cooperating with them.[41]

The advent of Khomeini heralded a constriction of religious pluralism to only forms of Shiite Islam. But the significant political evolution of "Khomeiniite" Shia included republican principles. Iran, under Khomeini's constitution, would be a theocratic Shiite republic, with Muslim male citizens, in good standing, voting for seats in Parliament.

In the process of creation of the various Pakistani constitutions, the first document, a "Magna Carta," to delineate constitutional rights was the Objectives Resolution, adopted in March 1949. The Resolution included a variety of provisions derived from Islamic exclusivism:

> Whereas sovereignty over the entire universe belongs to God Almighty alone, and the authority which He has delegated to the State of Pakistan through its people for being exercised within the limits prescribed by Him is a sacred trust;
>
> Wherein the principles of democracy, freedom, equality, tolerance and social justice, as enunciated by Islam shall be fully observed;
>
> Wherein the Muslims shall be enabled to order their lives in the individual and collective spheres in accord

---

41. John L. Esposito and John O. Voll, *Islam and Democracy* (1996), 47.

with the teaching and requirements of Islam as set out in the Holy Quran and the Sunna;

Wherein adequate provision shall be made for the minorities freely to profess and practice their religions and develop their cultures.[42]

The first actual constitution, the Constitution of 1956, provided that the President must be a Muslim,[43] Qur'anic education be compulsory,[44] and Islamic moral standards[45] be promoted. Article 27, however, provided for representation of minorities on the Federal and Provincial Services and that minorities could not be discriminated against.[46] Further, Article 156 provided a "Commission would be set up for making recommendations for bringing existing law into conformity with the Injunctions of Islam.[47]

The Constitution of 1962 replaced a provision in the 1956 version that ascribed the Qur'an and Sunna as the source of all law with an amendment that ascribed Islam as the source of all law.[48] The Constitution of 1973 was essentially the same on religious liberty but did not provide for the reconstruction of the Islamic Research Institute.[49]

Islamization begun in force under General Zhia in 1977, culminated with the Revival of the Constitution Order of 1985. The most Islamicized constitution to date, it yet allows for ten seats for minority religions, spread among Christian, Hindu, Sikh, Buddhist, Parsi, and Ahmadi constituents.[50] Other members of the

---

42. Rubya Mehdi, *The Islamization of the Law in Pakistan* (1994), 72–73.
43. Pakistani Constitution, Part IV, Art. 32(2) (1956).
44. Pakistani Constitution, Art. 25 (2)(b) (1956).
45. Pakistani Constitution, Art. 25 (2)(a) (1956).
46. Rubya Mehdi, *The Islamization of the Law in Pakistan* (1994), 83.
47. Tanzil-Ur-Rahman, *Islamization of Pakistan Law* (1978), 1.
48. Rubya Mehdi, *The Islamization of the Law in Pakistan* (1994), 90.
49. Mehdi, 100.
50. Pakistani Constitution Order, Art. 51 (1985).

Parliament[51] must be practicing Muslims.[52] The Preamble of each of the constitutions includes ascription of all-inclusive sovereignty to God and the people[53]—an ambiguity designed to appease both modernist and traditionalist.[54]

Western Sources for Article 35 of the Kuwaiti Constitution

When the ruling Amir in 1961 convened a constitutional convention to usher Kuwait's entrance into the family of nations, the commissioning implied drafting of a document respectable to the West. Accordingly, phraseology smacks of Western values, including Madisonian separation of powers and Lockean religious pluralism. This phraseology, however, merely veneer, is like felt over a fist, the fist of all executive, legislative, and judicial power residing in the Amir.

Comparison with Similar Provisions in Constitutions of Other Islamic States

In Turkey, for instance, "Everyone has the right to express or spread his thoughts and opinions... whether as an individual or as a group" (Article 26, Turkish Constitution). In Egypt, the Egyptian Constitution articulates Islam as the higher source of law in Egypt, higher than any secular provisions.[55] In Mauritania, according to

---

51. Pakistani Constitution Order, Art. 62 (e) (f) (1985).

52. See Mehdi,106.

53. See generally Tayyab Mahmud, "Praetorianism and Common Law in Post-Colonial Settings: Judicial Responses to Constitutional Breakdowns in Pakistan," 1993 *Utah L. Rev.* (1993),1225, 1273 n. 228 (exploring the adjudication of various courts grappling with conflicts between secular law and Islamic law).

54. Mehdi, 97.

55. "The New International Holy Alliance and the Struggle to Appropriate and Censor General Cultural Symbols, Speech, Religious Discrimination, and Blasphemy," 83 *Am. Soc'y Int'l L. Proc.* (April 5–8, 1989): 427, 434.

the Constitutional Charter, Islam is the state religion and the only source of law.[56]

CONCLUSION

Article 35, in isolation, appears to honor the Western value of religious pluralism. In both context and practice, however, Article 35 guarantees the "absolute" freedom of religion to Muslims only, particularly Sunni and Shiites loyal to the Amir. Ultimately in Kuwait, "freedom" is whatever the Amir makes it.

---

56. Mauritanian Charter preamble.

ISLAMIC DIVINE LAW'S (SHARIA) CAPITAL PUNISHMENT UPON APOSTASY DENIES THE INALIENABLE HUMAN RIGHT TO CHOOSE ONE'S BELIEFS

PROPOSED SOLUTIONS TO THE PROBLEM OF HONORING THE HUMAN RIGHTS OF KUWAITI MUSLIMS WHO CHANGE THEIR RELIGION

TOWARD AN ISLAMIC IDEOLOGICAL BASIS FOR RELIGIOUS TOLERATION IN KUWAIT

Qur'anic Passages Implying Religious Totalitarianism

A variety of Qur'anic passages establish the superiority and exclusivity of Islam. The more extreme elements in the Islamic community infer from these passages a warrant for persecution of non-Muslims:[1]

---

1. Masudul Hasan, *Reconstruction of Political Thought in Islam* (1988), 36–37.

ISLAMIC DIVINE LAW'S (SHARIA) CAPITAL PUNISHMENT

Sura 3:19: "The only religion before God is Islam."

Sura 3:38: "Do not seek a religion other than the religion of Islam."

Sura 3:85: "If one desires a religion other than Islam, never will it be accepted of him."

Sura 3:110: "The Muslims are the best peoples evolved for mankind."

Sura 5:5: "This Day have I perfected for, your religion, completed My favour to you, and chosen for you Islam as your religion."

Sura 4:125: "Who can be better than one who accepts Islam."

Sura 13:15: "Whatever things there are in the heavens and on earth prostrate themselves to God in Islam."

Sura 48:28: "Allah has sent His Apostle with Guidance and the religion of truth (Islam) to proclaim above all other religions."

Sura 72:14: "Those who surrender to God in Islam, they have sought out the path of right conduct."

Accordingly, a theology derived solely from passages such as these may incline toward oppression. Counterbalancing the assertions of exclusivity and superiority, the Qur'an, however, includes a demonstrable vein of toleration.

Qur'anic Passages Implying Religious Toleration

The following Qur'anic excerpts establish toleration as an acceptable Islamic norm. Perhaps if John Locke[2] read the Qur'an, he

---

2. See generally John Locke, *The Reasonableness of Christianity* (I. Ramsey ed. 1958) (1st ed. 1695); John Locke, *A Letter Concerning Toleration* (John Horton & Susan Mendus eds., 1990); Raymond Klibansky, *Preface to John Locke, Epistola de Tolerantia [Letter on Toleration]* passim (1968); John Marshall, *John Locke: Resistance, Religion and Responsibility* (1994); see Sandler, "Lockean Ideas in Thomas Jefferson's Bill for Establishing Religious Freedom,"

could find common ground for his political philosophy of religious toleration[3] in the following texts:

Sura 2:256: "There is no compulsion in religion."

Sura 3:176: "let not those grieve thee who rush headlong into Unbelief: not the least harm will they do to Allah: Allah's Plan is that He will give them no portion in the Hereafter, but a severe punishment."

Sura 6:104: "Now have come to you, from your Lord proofs (to open your eyes); If any will see, it will be (for the good of) his own soul: If any will be blind, it will be to his own (harm)."

Sura 6:108: "Do not revile those who call mankind [to worship] others than God, lest they [in turn] revile God out of ignorance and spite; for We [God] have made their own behaviour seem good to each community. At the end they must return to their Lord, and He will make them understand all they were doing."

Sura 6:109: "[t]o you be your Way [Religion], and to me mine."

Sura 10:99: "It had been thy Lord's Will, they would have believed, all who are on earth. Wilt thou then compel mankind against their will to believe?"

---

21 *J. Hist. Ideas* (1960): 100; see W. Berns, *The First Amendment and the Future of American Democracy*, (1985), 18–24 (tracing Jefferson's reliance upon Locke's first *Letter Concerning Toleration* in drafting Virginia's Bill for Establishing Religious Freedom); see Kessler, "Locke's Influence on Jefferson's 'Bill for Establishing Religious Freedom,'" 26 *J. Church & ST.* (1983): 231 (paralleling similarities between Locke's *Letters* and Jefferson's bill).

3. See generally, for example, Lino J. Lauro & Peter A. Samuelson, "Toward Pluralism in Sudan: A Traditionalist Approach," 37 *HARV. INT'L L.J.* (1996): 65 (arguing for the benefits of traditional pluralism over the religious "purism"); Dr. Hesham El-Essawy, chairperson of the Islamic Society for the Promotion of Religious Tolerance, claims that the Ayatollah's death sentence upon Salman Rushdie does not affect 95 percent of the world's Muslims. Diana Hinds, "Rushdie: Speech Puts Author 'in Greater Danger,'" *The Independent*, December 16, 1991, at 4.

ISLAMIC DIVINE LAW'S (SHARIA) CAPITAL PUNISHMENT

Sura 10:108-09: "Now Truth has reached you from your Lord! Those, who receive Guidance, do so for the good of their own souls; those who stray, do so to their own loss: And I [Muhammad] am not (set) over to arrange your affairs. Follow the inspiration sent unto thee, and be patient and constant, till Allah, do decide; for He is the Best to decide."

Sura 11:118: "If the Lord had so willed, He could have made mankind one single community; but they will still differ."

Sura 16:125: "[O Prophet] invite (all) to the Way of they Lord with wisdom and beautiful preaching; And argue with them in ways that are best and most gracious: For thy Lord knoweth best, who have strayed from His Path, and who receive guidance."

Sura 17:107: "You may believe in it [the Qur'an] or not."

Sura 18:29: "Say, Truth is from your Lord; let him who will, believe, and let him who will reject [Truth]."

Sura 22:68-69: "If they do wrangle with thee [O Muhammad], say: 'God knows best what it is ye are doing.' God will judge between you on the Day of Judgment concerning the matters on which ye differ."

Sura 30:22: "Among His signs is the creation of the heavens and the earth, and the variations in your languages and your colours."

Sura 39:41: "Verily we have the Book [the Holy Qu'ran] to thee in Truth, for (instructing) mankind. He, then, that receives guidance benefits his own soul: But he that strays injures his own soul. Nor art thou [Muhammad] set a custodian over them."

Sura 49:13: "O mankind! We [God] created you from a single pair of a male and a female, and have made you into nations and tribes, so that you might come to know one another. Verily the most honoured in the sight of God is [the one who is] the most deeply conscious of Him . . ."

Sura 88:21-26: "Therefore do thou give admonition, for thou are one to admonish, though thou are not to manage [men's] affairs. But if any turn away and reject God, God will punish him with a mighty punishment. For to Us [God] will be their return; then it will be for Us to call them to account."[4]

These Qur'anic passages imply that external coercion is not the designated means of evangelization or discipline of apostates.

A Qur'anic Theology of Toleration

A Summary of the Theology of Toleration in the Qur'an

The most pointed Qur'anic passage establishing religious toleration is Sura 2:256, stating that in religion there is no compulsion. Developing the principle are Sura 17:107 and 18:29, which allow practicing Muslims to allow others freedom of choice to accept or reject Islam. Sura 10:99 mitigates a rebuke by means of a rhetorical question—Muslims must not compel individuals to believe against their will. A Muslim is commanded to speak to a non-Muslim with wisdom and kindness in Sura 16:125. Actually, differences are divinely willed in Sura 11:118. In Sura 88:21-26, punishment for rejection of Islam is left to God alone.

Pure Qur'anic Theology Does Not Prescribe Capital Punishment for Muslims Who Change Their Religion

Roy Mottahedeh, Professor at Harvard, sees an Islamic theology of toleration. According to Mottahedeh, a Qur'anic base for religious toleration includes three maxims: the principle that differences are divinely willed; the principle that judgment and punishment for wrong belief are to be left to God alone; and the principle of

---

4. Syed Muzaffar-Ud-Din Hadvi, *Human Rights and Obligations (in Light of Quran and Hadith)* (1987), 42, citing, "Whoever kills a Dhimmi [a non-Muslim living in an Islamic State], shall not get [or smell] the odour of . . . Paradise, though it is smelt from a distance of forty year's journey."

mutuality of respect by human communities of belief.[5] Although apostasy appears thirteen times in the Qur'an,[6] all the verses assure that retribution lies with Allah in the afterlife.[7] Preceding the Hadith, the Qur'an is the first fundament of the Islamic religion. Its precedence should establish a practiced theology of toleration among its adherents.

Various Muslim Human-Rights Organizations Seek Enforcement of the Qur'anic Toleration Passages in Islamic Countries

The theology of toleration espoused in the Qur'an motivates a variety of Muslim human-rights organizations. Elizabeth Ann Mayer defends these NGos which see human rights as a part of, rather contrary to, pure Islam:

> Muslims who support the universality of human rights view with profound skepticism governments' appeals to Islam to justify their human rights violations. The views of such Muslims deserve to be considered before jumping to the conclusion that it is Islamic culture that is being assaulted and insulted when Western nations or international organizations decry governmental human

---

5. Roy Mottahedeh, "Toward an Islamic Theology of Toleration" in Lindholm, Tore and Kari Vogt (eds.) (Copenhagen: Nordic Human Rights Publications), 22–36; Compare Amir Ali, *The Spirit of Islam* (1974) (arguing that Islam enshrines tolerance more than other religions); see generally Ishtiaq Ahmed, *The Concept of an Islamic State: An Analysis of the Ideological Controversy in Pakistan* (1987) (exploring possible models for an Islamic state and the extent to which the divine law, as codified in the Shari'a, should be incorporated); "Objectives Resolution" (1949), in Safdar Mahmood, *Constitutional Foundations of Pakistan*, (2d rev. ed. 1990), 46.

6. S.A. Rahman, *The Punishment of Apostasy in Islam* (1972), 1–8.

7. See Hazrat Tahir Ahmad, *Murder in the Name of Allah* (1989), 74–92; Muhammad Zafrulla Khan, *Punishment of Apostasy in Islam* (London Mosque n.d.), 24–33. Explaining that there is no punishment for apostasy according to Islam: "Let not those grieve thee who rush headlong into Unbelief: not the least harm will they do to Allah: Allah's Plan is that He will give them no portion in the Hereafter, but a severe punishment," Sura 3:176.

rights violations and call for the universal observance of international human rights norms.

Far from charging Western nations and international organizations with cultural insensitivity, independent human-rights organizations in the Middle East have encouraged outsiders to criticize human-rights violations and to express support for their domestic initiatives on behalf of human rights, and they have collaborated with international human-rights organizations[8] that are likewise committed to international norms.[9]

Over fifty distinguished Muslim jurists and political philosophers convened in Kuwait to frame a statement on human rights in Islamic countries.[10] The Universal Islamic Declaration of Human Rights, adopted by the Islamic Council in 1981, includes provisions that smack of a variety of international declarations guaranteeing protection of human rights:

> Article X, "Rights of Minorities": The Qur'anic principle 'there is no compulsion in religion' shall govern the religious rights of non-Muslim countries. In a Muslim country, religious minorities shall have the choice to be governed in respect of their civil and personal matters by Islamic Law or by their own laws.

Further, Article XIII allows every person the right to freedom of conscience and worship in accordance with one's religious beliefs. Article XIII(e) forbids ridiculing, holding in contempt, or inciting public hostility against the religious beliefs of others.

---

8. Donna E. Arzt, "The Application of International Human Rights Law in Islamic States." *Human Rts. Quart.* 12 (1990): 202.

9. Ann Elizabeth Mayer, "Universal Versus Islamic Human Rights: A Clash of Cultures or a Clash with a Construct?" 15 *Mich. J. Int'l. L.* (1994): 307, 364.

10. See International Comm'n of Jurists, "Human Rights in Islam" (1982).

ISLAMIC DIVINE LAW'S (SHARIA) CAPITAL PUNISHMENT

TOWARD HONORING THE IDEALS OF INTERNATIONAL CONVENTIONS IN KUWAIT

The Foundational Principle of International Law

The foundational principle of international law is national sovereignty.[11] Thus, the crux of the U.N. Charter[12] is "the principle of the sovereign equality of all its Members."[13] Accordingly, any foreign policy must respect national autonomy, recognizing the right of a nation to govern itself. International conventions, as articulated in various declarations, demonstrate a consensus that individuals should have the functional right to choose their own religion. U.S. posture toward Kuwait should include respect for Kuwaiti national autonomy balanced by expression of concern for religious liberty. The Iranian regime, for instance, claims that the West uses human rights as a "pretext for interfering in its internal affairs" after Western protests against Iran's expulsion of the International Red Cross.[14] But both national autonomy and religious liberty are worthy values to shape U.S. foreign policy.

Specific International Conventions Codified

The following précis of excerpts from various international declarations demonstrates a consensus of international belief that individuals should have the right to choose their own religion.

---

11. Paul W. Kahn, "Lessons for International Law from the Gulf War," 45 STAN.L.REV. (1993), 425, 435.

12. See generally Kahn, 425 (1993) (exploring the conflicting values of respect for national sovereignty and respect for human rights).

13. U.N. Charter, art. 2 ¶1.

14. See Peter Feuilherade, "Iran: An Astute Move," *Middle E. Int'l.* (June 11, 1993): 11.

United Nations' General Assembly Resolution on the Declaration for the Elimination of All Forms of Intolerance and of Discrimination Based on Religion and Belief

The United Nations' General Assembly Resolution on the Declaration for the Elimination of All Forms of Intolerance and of Discrimination Based on Religion and Belief[15] is the most relevant U.N. declaration to the issue of religious liberty in Kuwait. The Declaration provides for freedom to manifest one's religion or belief, including non-religious belief, but also that freedom may be subject to limitations prescribed by law which are necessary to protect public safety, order, health, or morals or the fundamental rights and freedoms of others:[16]

> Considering that religion or belief, for anyone who professes either, is one of the fundamental elements in his conception of life and that freedom of religion or belief should be fully respected and guaranteed, Considering that it is essential to promote understanding, tolerance and respect in matters relating to freedom of religion and belief and to ensure that the use of religion or belief for ends inconsistent with the Charter, other relevant instruments of the United Nations and the purposes and principles of the present Declaration is inadmissible, Convinced that freedom of religion and belief should also contribute to the attainment of the goals of world peace, social justice and friendship among peoples and to the elimination of ideologies or practices of colonialism and racial discrimination . . .[17]

Further, Article One, Section One provides for freedom of thought and expression both in private and public:

---

15. United Nations: General Assembly Resolution on the Declaration for the Elimination of All Forms of Intolerance and of Discrimination Based on Religion and Belief, U.N. General Assembly Resolution 36/55, adopted November 25, 1981. WESTLAW 21 *I.L.M.* (1982): 205.
16. Ibid.
17. Ibid.

Article One, Section One: Everyone shall have the right to freedom of thought, conscience and religion. This right shall include freedom to have a religion or whatever belief of his choice, and freedom, either individually or in community with other and in public or private, to manifest his religion or belief in worship, observance, practice and teaching.[18]

The second and third sections of Article One forbid coercion to limit, curb, or influence religious belief, except reasonable limitations that are necessary for public health or morals:

Article One, Section Two: No one shall be subject to coercion which would impair his freedom to have a religion or belief of his choice.[19]

Article One, Section Three: Freedom to manifest one's religion or beliefs may be subject only to such limitations as are prescribed by law and are necessary to protect public safety, order, health or morals or the fundamental rights and freedoms of others.[20]

The Second Article of the Declaration attacks discrimination on the basis of religion as a demonstrable evil:

Article Two, Section One: No one shall be subject to discrimination by any State, institution, group or persons or person on the grounds of religion or other beliefs.[21]

Article Two, Section Two: For the purposes of the present Declaration, the expression "intolerance and discrimination based on religion or belief" means any distinction, exclusion, restriction or preference based on religion or belief and having as its purpose or as its effect nullification or impairment of the recognition, enjoyment or

18. Ibid.
19. Ibid.
20. Ibid.
21. United Nations: General Assembly Resolution on the Declaration for the Elimination of All Forms of Intolerance and of Discrimination Based on Religion and Belief, U.N. General Assembly Resolution 36/55, adopted November 25, 1981. WESTLAW 21 *I.L.M.* (1982): 205

exercise of human rights and fundamental freedoms on an equal basis.

The third article of the Declaration applies the common ground of the Charter of the United Nations, the Universal Declaration on Human Rights, and the International Covenants on Human Rights:

> Article Three, Section One: Discrimination between human beings on the grounds of religion or belief constitutes an affront to human dignity and a disavowal of the principles of the Charter of the United Nations, and shall be condemned as a violation of the human rights and fundamental freedoms proclaimed in the Universal Declaration on Human Rights and enunciated in detail in the International Covenants on Human Rights, and as an obstacle to friendly and peaceful relations between nations.[22]

The fourth article of the Declaration aims at the rescission of legislation that discriminates on the basis of religious belief:

> Article Four, Section One: All States shall take effective measures to prevent and eliminate discrimination on the grounds of religion or belief in the recognition, exercise and enjoyment of human rights and fundamental freedoms in all fields of civil, economic, political, social and cultural life.[23]

> Article Four, Section Two: All States shall make all efforts to rescind legislation where necessary to prohibit any such discrimination, and to take all appropriate measures to combat intolerance on the grounds of religions or other beliefs in this matter.[24]

Article Six of the Declaration specifically provides for the free exchange of religious ideas:

---

22. Ibid.
23. Ibid.
24. Ibid.

Article Six: (T)he right to freedom of thought, conscience, religion or belief shall include, inter alia, the following freedoms: (a) To worship or assemble in connection with a religion or belief, and to establish and maintain places for these purposes; (b) To establish and maintain appropriate charitable and humanitarian institutions; . . . (d) To write, issue and disseminate relevant publications in these areas; (e) To teach a religion or belief in places suitable for these purposes.[25]

Application of the Declaration to Kuwait would "broadside" the Kuwaiti Constitution's provision of shari'a as a main source of legislation unless the Qur'an is interpreted to allow for freedom of religion, relaxing the exclusivity of shari'a.[26]

An International Consensus, as Represented by International Declarations, Exists That Choosing One's Religion Is a Fundamental Right

The United Nations General Assembly adopted the International Covenant on Civil and Political Rights unanimously on December 16, 1966. The Covenant entered into p 87 force on March 23, 1976. The U.S., under President Carter, signed the Covenant on October 5, 1977.[27] The Senate voted its advice and consent to ratification of the Covenant on April 2, 1992 and on June 8, 1992, the United States deposited its instrument of ratification. The Covenant entered into force for the United States on September 8, 1992.[28]

The Covenant undertakes to procure "rights guaranteed," including "freedom of thought, conscience, and religion; freedom of

---

25. Ibid.

26. See generally Donna E. Arzt, "The Application of International Human Rights Law in Islamic States," *Human Rts. Quart.* 12(1990), 202.

27. Westlaw 31 *I.L.M.* (1992), 645, 648.

28. United States: Senate Committee on Foreign Relations Report on the International Covenant on Civil and Political Rights, U.S. Senate Executive Report (102d Cong., 2d Sess.), 102–23. Westlaw, 31 *I.L.M.* (1992), 645.

expression; right of peaceful assembly; freedom of association."[29] Further, the Covenant undertakes "to respect and to ensure" to all individuals within its territory and under its jurisdiction the rights recognized in the Covenant "without distinction of any kind, such as race, color, sex, language, religion, political or other opinion, national or social origin, property, birth or other status"; to adopt legislative or other measures necessary to give effect to these rights; and to provide an effective remedy to those whose rights are violated."[30] Rights enumerated include "non-discrimination" and "equal protection."[31]

Another international document presupposing liberty of conscience derives from the U.N.'s Conference on Women. The U.N. Fourth World Conference on Women deliberated upon and drafted a forthright resolution, the United Nations Fourth World Conference on Women: Declaration and Platform for Action, acknowledging the right of religious freedom for both men and women:

> Religion, spirituality and belief play a central role in the lives of millions of women and men, in the way they live and in the aspirations they have for the future. The right to freedom of thought, conscience and religion is inalienable and must be universally enjoyed. This right includes the freedom to have or to adopt the religion or belief of their choice either individually or in community with others, in public or in private, and to manifest their religion or belief in worship, observance, practice and teaching. In order to realize equality, development and peace, there is a need to respect these rights and freedoms fully. Religion, thought, conscience and belief may, and can contribute to fulfilling women's and men's

---

29. Article Five—Major Provisions; Section 1—"Rights Guaranteed: The International Covenant on Civil and Political Rights," Westlaw 31 *I.L.M.* (1992), 645, 650.

30. Ibid.

31. Ibid.

moral, ethical and spiritual needs and to realizing their full potential in society.[32]

The Declaration correctly affirms fulfillment of spiritual needs as vital to achievement of one's full potential in society.

Another international pact involving the United Kingdom, Zimbabwe, and Rhodesia[33] articulates a theory of liberty of conscience. The declaration derives from the moral philosophy that conscience is sacred:

> Article Eight—"Freedom of Conscience"; Section (1): It will be forbidden, except with the consent of the person concerned, to interfere with anybody's freedom of conscience. This freedom will be defined as including freedom of thought and of religion, freedom to change one's religion or belief, and freedom, either alone or in community with others, and in both public and in private, to manifest and propagate one's religion or belief or worship, teaching, practice and observance.[34]

> Article Eight—"Freedom of Conscience"; Section (2): It will be forbidden to prevent any religious community from providing religious instruction for members of that community in the course of any education which it provides.[35]

> Article Eight—"Freedom of Conscience"; Section (3): It will also be forbidden, except with the consent of the person concerned or his guardian, to require any person attending a place of education to receive religious p 90 instruction, or to take part in a religious observance, except when it relates to his own religion.[36]

---

32. United Nations Fourth World Conference on Women: "Declaration and Platform for Action," September 15, 1995, Article 24, page 37.

33. "Zimbabwe Rhodesia—United Kingdom: Agreements Concluded at Lancaster House Conference," Westlaw 19 *I.L.M.* (1980), 387.

34. Ibid.

35. Ibid.

36. Ibid.

The limitations placed upon liberty of conscience are reasonable societal demands:

> Article Eight—"Freedom of Conscience"; Section (5): There will be an exception to the foregoing for any law (or for any measures taken under it) which makes reasonable provision in the interests of defense, public safety, public order, public morality or public health; or which makes reasonable provision for the purpose of protecting the rights and freedoms of others, including their freedom from unsolicited interference by persons of other religions or beliefs. Any such law (and the measures taken under it) will be tested against the criterion of what would be reasonably justifiable in a democratic society.[37]

The declaration specifically forbids interference with religious practice:

> Article Nine—"Freedom of Expression"; Section (1): It will be forbidden, except with the consent of the person concerned, to interfere with anybody's freedom of expression. This freedom will be defined as including freedom to hold opinions without interference, freedom to receive ideas and information without interference, freedom to communicate ideas and information without interference and freedom from interference with one's correspondence."[38]

This declaration accurately expresses an underlying value of common law theory.

The tragic holocaust in Cambodia sparked the Paris Conference[39] to establish some semblance of domestic tranquility. The opening line of Annex 5, "Principles for a New Constitution

---

37. Ibid.

38. "Zimbabwe Rhodesia—United Kingdom: Agreements Concluded at Lancaster House Conference," Westlaw 19 *I.L.M.* (1980): 387, 391.

39. "Paris Conference on Cambodia: Agreements Elaborating the Framework for a Comprehensive Political Settlement of the Cambodia Conflict," Paris, October 23, 1991, reproduced from U.N. Document A/46/608, S/23177, October 30, 1991, Westlaw 31 *I.L.M.* (1992): 174.

ISLAMIC DIVINE LAW'S (SHARIA) CAPITAL PUNISHMENT

for Cambodia," Paragraph 2, is an understatement: "Cambodia's tragic recent history requires special measures to assure protection of human rights." Annex 5 offers constitutional direction to the suffering fledgling nation:

> Therefore, the constitution will contain a declaration of fundamental rights, including the rights to life, personal liberty, security, freedom of movement, freedom of religion, assembly and association including political parties and trade unions, due process and equality before the law, protection from arbitrary deprivation of property or deprivation of private property without just compensation, and freedom from racial, ethnic, religious or sexual discrimination . . .[40]

Forthrightly, the Paris Conference establishes religious liberty as an imperative premium.

The tragic violence in Bosnia also sparked an international conference, which drafted the General Framework Agreement for Peace.[41] Article Two, Paragraph Two, of the declaration articulates fundamental freedoms in general, but Paragraph Three specifically ensures "freedom of thought, conscience, and religion":

> Article Two—"Human Rights and Fundamental Freedoms"; Paragraph 3—"Enumeration of Rights": All persons within the territory of Bosnia and Herzegovina shall enjoy the human rights and fundamental freedoms referred to in paragraph 2 above; these include: (g) Freedom of thought, conscience, and religion; (h) Freedom of expression; (i) Freedom of peaceful assembly and freedom of association with others.[42]

In a place of armed hostilities motivated by religious differences the declaration sings a Siren song of peace.

---

40. "Paris Conference on Cambodia," Westlaw, 174, 200.

41. "Bosnia and Herzegovina-Croatia-Yugoslavia: General Framework Agreement for Peace in Bosnia and Herzegovina with Annexes," Paris, December 14, 1995, Westlaw 35 *I.L.M.* (1996): 75, 119.

42. Ibid.

INTERNATIONAL LAW AFLOAT ON A SEA OF WORLD RELIGIONS

Even a pact established between Israel and the Papacy[43] underscores the valued premium of religious freedom. Israel vowed respect for "freedom of religion and conscience" according to its own Declaration of Independence and the international instruments to which it is a signatory:

> Article 1, Paragraph 1, The State of Israel, recalling its Declaration of Independence, affirms its continuing commitment to uphold and observe the human right to freedom of religion and conscience, as set forth in the Universal Declaration of Human Rights and in other international instruments to which it is a party.[44]

The Vatican echoed its similar commitment to respect the "freedom of religion and conscience":

> Article 1, Paragraph 2, The Holy See, recalling the Declaration on Religious Freedom of the Second Vatican Ecumenical Council, 'Dignitatis humanea', affirms the Catholic Church's commitment to uphold the human right to freedom of religion and conscience, as set forth in the Universal Declaration of Human Rights and in other international instruments to which it is a party. The Holy See wishes to affirm as well the Catholic Church's respect for other religions and their followers as solemnly stated by the Second Vatican Council in its Declaration on the Relation of the Church to Non-Christian Religions,' Nostra aetate'.[45]

The Israeli/Vatican agreement demonstrates the international communitarian effort to honor human dignity[46] by respecting liberty of conscience.

---

43. "Holy See-Israel: Fundamental Agreement," December 30, 1993, Westlaw 33 *I.L.M.* (1994): 153.

44. "Holy See-Israel": 153, 154.

45. Ibid.

46. See also "Universal Declaration on Human Rights," General Assembly resolution 217 A (III); "International Covenants on Human Rights," General Assembly resolution 2200 A (XXI), annex. [see Westlaw 6 *I.L.M.* (1967)]: 360; Article 9, "Freedom of Thought, Conscience and Religion"; Article 10, "Freedom of Expression"; Article 11, "Freedom of Assembly and Association";

ISLAMIC DIVINE LAW'S (SHARIA) CAPITAL PUNISHMENT

"Council of Europe: Explanatory Report and Protocol No. 11 to the Convention for the Protection of Human Rights and Fundamental Freedoms, Restructuring the Control Machinery Established Thereby," Strasbourg, May 11, 1994, Westlaw 33 *I.L.M.* (1994): 943, 967; "European Court of Human Rights: Judgment in Young, James and Webster Case (British Rail Closed-Shop Agreement; Refusal to Join Trade Union; Freedom of Association)," August 13, 1981, 21 *I.L.M.* (1982): 577 (affirming the "freedom of thought, of conscience or of religion"); United Nations: Convention on the Rights of the Child, in force December 5, 1989, adopted without vote November 20, 1989, reproduced from the U.N. General Assembly Document A/RES/44/25, Westlaw 28 *I.L.M.* (1989): 1448, 1450 fn. 18 (explaining the "freedom of religion" for children remains a "hot topic" or "highly controversial"); "Italy—The Holy See: Agreement to Amend the 1929 Lateran Concordat," Rome, February 18, 1984, 24 *I.L.M.* (1985): 1589 (affirming the independence of church and state and "the principles of freedom of religion"); "U.S. Helsinki Watch Committee Reports on 1986 Violations of the Helsinki Accords in Nine Countries," 26 *I.L.M.*: 598, "The reports concentrate on recent violations to the Accords and consider the major categories of the human rights provisions of the Helsinki Accords—freedom of expression, freedom of association, freedom of movement and freedom of religion." "The reports conclude that while Poland, Czechoslovakia and Hungary allow some degree of human rights, the U.S.S.R. is the most oppressive, followed by Rumania and Turkey"; Article 18 of the International Covenant on Civil and Political Rights provides for freedom of religion. The limitation on this provision is paragraph 3, which permits restrictions on religious expression should public morals or public order warrant. "The New International Holy Alliance and the Struggle to Appropriate and Censor General Cultural Symbols, Speech, Religious Discrimination, and Blasphemy," 83 *AM. SOC'Y. INT'L L. PROC.* (April 5-8, 1989): 427, 434; "Conference on Security and Cooperation in Europe: Concluding Document from the Vienna Meeting," November 4, 1986–January 17, 1989, 28 *I.L.M.* (1989): 527 (holding that "the participating States recognize that the exercise of the above mentioned rights relating to the freedom of religion or belief may be subject only to such limitations as are provided by law and consistent with their obligations under international law and with their international commitments. They will ensure in their laws and regulations and in their application the full and effective implementation of the freedom of thought, conscience, religion or belief . . .'"; Part II. "Human Rights and Fundamental Freedoms," A. General, Article 2. "Bosnia and Herzegovina: Constitution of the Federation," March 18, 1994, 33 *I.L.M.* (1994): 740 (codifying that "all persons within the territory of the Federation shall enjoy the rights (d) To freedom from discrimination based on race, color, sex, language, religion or creed, political or other opinions, and national or social origin" and (l) "To fundamental freedoms: free speech and press; freedom of thought, conscience, and belief; freedom of religion, including private and public worship; freedom of assembly; freedom of association,

Additionally, a variety of U.S. unilateral declarations, including the Foreign Relations Authorization Act, Fiscal Years 1988 and 1989,[47] demonstrate the U.S. resolve against persecution on religious grounds:

> Section 1204—"United States Policy against Persecution of Christians in Eastern Europe and the Soviet Union," "International Organizations," Paragraph (2): the governments of the Union of Soviet Socialist Republics and Eastern European countries should comply with their commitments under the United Nations Universal Declaration of Human Rights, the International Covenants

---

including to form and belong to and labor unions and the freedom not to associate; and freedom to work"); "People's Republic of China: The Basic Law of Hong Kong Special Administrative Region of the People's Republic of China," April 4, 1990 WESTLAW 29 *I.L.M.*: 1511, 1517 (codifying in Chapter VI, Articles 136-149, "Hong Kong shall: Retain academic autonomy and freedom of religion; improve medical and health services; provide protection of intellectual property; not restrict freedom of religion; establish qualifications for profession; formulate sports policy; improve the social welfare system; formulate labor law and policy; not interfere with non-governmental organizations"); "Conference on Security and Cooperation in Europe: Charter of Paris for a New Europe and Supplementary Document to Give Effect to Certain Provisions of the Charter," Paris, November 21, 1990) WESTLAW 30 *I.L.M.* (1990): 190, 194 (testifying, "We affirm that, without discrimination, every individual has the right to: freedom of thought, conscience and religion or belief, freedom of expression, freedom of association and peaceful assembly, freedom of movement"); "Canada-European Communities-France-Federal Republic of Germany-Italy-Japan-United Kingdom-United States: Declaration on Human Rights and Economic Declaration from the Paris Economic Summit," July 15-16, 1989, reproduced from the *U.S. Weekly Compilation of Presidential Documents,* Volume 25, no. 29 (July 24, 1989), 1109-09 Westlaw 28 *I.L.M.*: 1282, 1293) (including "we stress the protection of freedom of thought, conscience and religion, and of freedom of opinion and expression; for without these freedoms, other rights cannot be fully realized" and "We believe equally in freedom of association in a pluralist society"); "U.N. Commission on Human Rights; Preliminary Report by the Special Representations on the Human Rights Situation in the Islamic Republic of Iran," U.N. GAOR, U.N.Doc. E/CN.4/1985/20 (1985): 13-19 (equating the prohibition against torture with a fundamental freedom, the level of "jus cogens," irrespective of race, sex, language, and religion).

47. December 22, 1987, reproduced from U.S. Public law 100-204 of December 22, 1987, Westlaw 27 *I.L.M.* (1988): 715.

on Human Rights, the Final Act of the Conference on Security and Cooperation in Europe, and the Madrid Concluding Document, and (3) the governments of the Union of Soviet Socialist Republics and Eastern European countries should immediately cease persecuting individuals on the basis of their faith and should afford Christians and other believers their internationally recognized right to freedom of religion.[48]

Violation of the right of religious self-determination is foreign to the framing values undergirding the U.S. Bill of Rights.

Liberty of thought, conscience, and religion are widely recognized as a fundamental human right. Jefferson's words were not the product of mere Judeo-Christian post-Enlightenment ideology: "I have sworn on the altar of God eternal hostility to all forms of tyranny over the mind of man."

TOWARD A PEACEFUL AND FRIENDLY RELATIONSHIP WITH THE UNITED STATES

The Carter Presidency marked an evolution in U.S. foreign policy[49] toward greater concern for human rights,[50] rather than

48. "United States: Foreign Relations Authorization Act, Fiscal Years 1988 and 1989," December 22, 1987, reproduced from U.S. Public law 100-204 of December 22, 1987, Westlaw 27 *I.L.M.* (1988): 715.

49. Compare, e.g., "United States: International Security and Development Cooperation Act of 1981," December 29, 1981, reproduced from U.S. Public Law 97-113, Westlaw 21 *I.L.M.* (1982): 172. On Nicaragua, Section 724 (a) "In furnishing assistance under this Act to the Government of Nicaragua, the President shall take into account the extent to which that Government has engaged in violations of internationally recognized human rights (including the right to organize and operate labor unions free from political oppression, the right to freedom of the press, and the right to freedom of religion) and shall encourage the Government of Nicaragua to respect those rights." "United States: International Security and Development Cooperation Act of 1981," December 29, 1981, reproduced from U.S. Public Law 97-113, Westlaw 21 *I.L.M.* (1982): 172.

50. See Harold Hongju Koh, "The 'Haiti Program' in United States Human Rights Policy—Symposium: The Informal Economy," 103 *YALE. L. J.* (1994): 2391 (explaining Carter's presidency the first to raise human-rights concerns

pure national self-interest. Ongoing concern for human rights in Kuwait is of moment for U.S. foreign policy because of the U.S. investment, with a literal deposit of life, in Kuwait's future.

The Integrity of the U.S.'s Moralistic Claims That Allegedly Motivated the Gulf War

The integrity of the U.S. to her ideology of liberty warrants ongoing influence toward human rights. The rhetoric of liberty, for instance, draped President Bush's speeches justifying the liberation of Kuwait. The day the air war commenced against Iraqi forces, January 16, 1991, President Bush declaimed:

> This is an historic moment. We have in this past year made great progress in ending the long era of conflict and cold war. We have before us the opportunity to forge for ourselves and for future generations a new world order, a world where the rule of law, not the law of the jungle, governs the conduct of nations.[51]

In a similar vein, Bush declaimed in the State of the Union Address on January 29, 1991:

---

above the level of rhetoric); see generally Frank Newman and David Weissbrodt, *International Human Rights* (1990), 502–44 (tracing the human-rights impetus for foreign policy in the presidencies of Franklin Delano Roosevelt, Woodrow Wilson, John F. Kennedy, and Jimmy Carter); Stephen B. Cohen, "Conditioning U.S. Security Assistance on Human Rights Practices," 76 *Am. J. Int'l. L.* (1982): 246 (outlining resistance of the executive bureaucracy to Carter-initiated human-rights concerns in U.S. foreign policy); Elizabeth F. Schwartz, "Getting Away With Murder: Social Cleansing in Colombia and the Role of the United States," 27 *Miami Inter-Am. L. Rev.* (1996), 381 (explaining human-rights concerns must be balanced with respect for national autonomy and self-determination, citing, for instance Underhill v. Hernandez, 168 U.S. (1897), 250, 252: "every sovereign State is bound to respect the independence of every other sovereign State, and the courts of one country will not sit in judgment on the acts of the government of another done within its own territory").

51. *New York Times*, January 17, 1991, A14, col. 1.

ISLAMIC DIVINE LAW'S (SHARIA) CAPITAL PUNISHMENT

> For two centuries, we've done the hard work of freedom. And tonight, we lead the world in facing down a threat to decency and humanity. What is at stake is more than one small country, it is a big idea: a new world order where diverse nations are drawn together in common cause to achieve the universal aspirations of mankind ... peace and security, freedom and the rule of law. Such is a world worthy of our struggle and worthy of our children's future ... Saddam Hussein's unprovoked invasion ... violated everything the community of nations holds dear."[52]

In the Democrat response, Senate Majority Leader George Mitchell echoed the rhetoric of liberty:

> Out of the tragedy of war, we seek a world where the force of law is more powerful than the force of arms. We seek a world where justice and human rights are respected everywhere. Students massacred in China, priests murdered in Central America, demonstrators gunned down in Lithuania—these acts of violence are as wrong as Iraqi soldiers killing civilians. We cannot oppose repression in one place an overlook it in another.[53]

Triumphantly, Bush declared victory for allied forces on February 27, 1991: "This is a victory for the United Nations, for all mankind, for the rule of law and for what is right."[54] In a joint session before Congress in early March 1991, Bush declared:

> a victory for the rule of law and for what is right. Until now, the world we've known has been a world divided— a world of barbed wire and concrete block, conflict and cold war. Now, we can see a new world coming into view. A world in which there is the very real prospect of a new world order. In the word of Winston Churchill, a "world order" in which "the principles of justice and fair play... protect the weak against the strong..." A world in which

---

52. *New York Times*, January 30, 1991, A12, col. 1.
53. *Washington Post*, January 30, 1991, A15, col. 1.
54. *New York Times*, February 28, 1991, A12, col. 1.

freedom and respect for human rights finds a home among all nations.[55]

The alleged ideological basis for the U.S. liberation of Kuwait warrant ongoing concern Kuwaiti human rights, including freedom of religion. Accordingly, the U.S. has a moral obligation to pursue enforcement of the alleged values that motivated the Gulf War. The four publicly declared U.S. objectives for the massive military operation were: (1) the immediate and unconditional withdrawal of all Iraqi troops from Kuwait; (2) the restoration of Kuwait's previous government; (3) security and stability of Saudi Arabia and the Persian Gulf; and (4) the protection of American citizens abroad.[56] But the second objective should now evolve to advance human rights in the restored government of Kuwait.

The U.N. Security Council provided, recalling its resolutions 660 and 661 (1990),

> gravely alarmed by the declaration by Iraq of a "comprehensive and eternal merger" with Kuwait; demanding, once again, that Iraq withdraw immediately and unconditionally all its forces to the positions in which they were located on 1 August 1990; determined to bring the occupation of Kuwait by Iraq to an end and to restore sovereignty, independence and territorial integrity of Kuwait; determined also to restore the authority of the legitimate Government of Kuwait; decides that annexation of Kuwait by Iraq under any form and whatever pretext has no legal validity, and it considered null and void; calls upon all states, international organizations, specialized agencies not to recognize that annexation, and to refrain from any action or dealing that might be interpreted as an indirect recognition of the annexation; further demands that Iraq rescind its action purporting to annex Kuwait; decides to keep this item on its

---

55. *New York Times*, March 7, 1991, A7, col. 1.

56. David J. Scheffer, "United Nations and International Law Are Flying High, But Real Test Is to Come, *Los Angeles Times*, September 2, 1990, M2.

agenda to continue its efforts to put an early end to the occupation.[57]

Kahn dissects the deontology of the U.S. commitment in a series of rhetorical questions:

> But why protect Kuwait? Kuwait, by anyone's standards, hardly embodied a just regime. Defending that regime did not mean protecting the human rights and self-determination of the Kuwaiti people. If that was not clear before the War, it has surely become clear in the War's aftermath. Was the goal of the War nothing more than the substitution of one unjust regime for another? One regime was domestic and the other foreign, but was this goal worth so much sacrifice and destruction? How many lives were worth sacrificing for the ruling family of Kuwait? When we ask this question from the perspective of international law, we cannot simply measure U.S. lives. Was Iraq's destruction worth the benefit to the international community of saving the Kuwait regime? Does the answer change if we define the goal as the saving of Kuwaiti sovereignty? Sovereignty is only a formal legal quality that may or may not—depending on the circumstances—support a morally valuable goal.[58]

Kahn correctly implies that the piercing question "For what did we fight?" should be a guiding compass to steer U.S. moral posture toward Kuwait.

The Enforcement of Shari'a's Capital Punishment upon Apostates an Obstacle to Full and Friendly Relations between the U.S. and Kuwait

The current Kuwaiti jurisprudence of capital punishment upon Muslims who change their religion is "an obstacle to friendly and peaceful relations" with the United States.

---

57. 9 I.L.M. 1(199): 323; see also "Resolution Says Iraq Must Reverse Step," *Washington Post*, August 10, 1990, A30, col. 1.

58. Kahn, 24–25.

Article Three, Section One: Discrimination between human beings on the grounds of religion or belief constitutes an affront to human dignity and a disavowal of the principles of the Charter of the United Nations, and shall be condemned as a violation of the human rights and fundamental freedoms proclaimed in the Universal Declaration on Human Rights and enunciated in detail in the International Covenants on Human Rights, and as an obstacle to friendly and peaceful relations between nations.[59]

Discrimination, a relative term, that devolves into the extreme of capital punishment for mere espousal of a religious belief posing no threat to public morals or security is a barrier to full and friendly relations between the U.S. and Kuwait.

TOWARD A KUWAITI RELAXATION OF RELIGIOUS EXCLUSIVISM

Deconstructing Islamic Provincialism on Human Rights

The Problem of Cultural Relativism

Prevailing values, varying from culture to culture, determine the extent of human rights in general, and freedom of religion in particular. For instance, Samuel P. Huntington, director of the Olin Institute for Strategic Studies at Harvard University, argues that freedom is a relative term,[60] determined by the religion and culture of Islam:

---

59. "United Nations: General Assembly Resolution on the Declaration for the Elimination of All Forms of Intolerance and of Discrimination Based on Religion and Belief," U.N. General Assembly Resolution 36/55, adopted November 25, 1981. Westlaw 21 *I.L.M.*: 205, 207.

60. Lawrence Rosen, *The Anthropology of Justice: Law as Culture in Islamic Society* (1989), critiqued in Ann E. Mayer, *Islam Inside and Out*, 22 J. *Interdisciplinary Hist.* (1991): 89 (positing a monolithic, anachronistic, and static Islamic culture which determines Muslim attitudes and behavior and distinguishes Islamic society from any counterpart in the West). In the same vein, see Sadiq Jalal al-'Azm, "Orientalism and Orientalism in Reverse," in *Forbidden*

Freedom is a concept defined within specific cultural and ideological boundaries. There is no universal definition of freedom. The problem we face is the demands by some religious and secular intellectual for freedom in its modern, humanist form in the environment created by a religious revolution.... Religion does not deny freedom, but its freedom starts with servitude to God. Accepting the means of interpreting freedom within the boundaries of shari'a ... and Islamic values ... in the Islamic shari'a, freedom of expression does not extend to the freedom to corrupt. The purpose of religion is to lead human beings to perfection; not everything can be permitted.[61]

Freedom in Islam derives from seeking Allah, the only entity in the universe that is entirely devoid of constraints—perfectly free.[62] Rebellion against Allah, therefore, is a loss of freedom.[63] To the Islamic mind, "the anarchy of liberal individualism cannot be a creative seedbed of culture."[64] Classic liberalism, oriented toward the individual, "see[s] social institutions as 'logical fictions,' possessing no existence beyond that of the individuals who collectively compose them."[65] The concept of freedom in Islam is foreign to the Western concept: "while in the liberal tradition freedom signifies the ability to act, in Islam it is the ability to exist."[66]

Agendas: Intolerance and Defiance in the Middle East (John Rothschild comp., 1984), 349, 367. Douglas Lee Donoho, "Relativism Versus Universalism in Human Rights: The Search for Meaningful Standards," 27 *Stan. J. Int'l. L.* (1991): 345, 353. Alison Dundes Rentln, *International Human Rights; Universalism Versus Relativism* (1990). Richard Falk, "Cultural Foundations for Protection of Human Rights," in *Human Rights in Cross-Cultural Perspectives: A Quest for Consensus* (Abdullahi An-Nim ed., 1992), 44.

61. Untitled essay, Shahriar Zarshenaz, in "Inside Iran," *Index on Censorship* (March 1992), 12.

62. Kimberly Younce Schooley, "Cultural Sovereignty, Islam, and Human Rights—Toward a Communitarian Revision," 25 *CUMB. L. REV.* (1995): 651, 694.

63. Ibid.
64. Ibid.
65. Ibid.
66. Ibid.

Western notions of freedom challenge the encrustation of custom as social debility:

> The despotism of custom is everywhere the standing hindrance to human advancement, being in unceasing antagonism to that disposition to aim at something better than customary, which is called, according to circumstances, the spirit of liberty, or that of progress or improvement.[67]

Culture, as much as religious principle, divides Islamic communities from internationally recognized human rights.

A Negative Precedent: International Convention Declared Null and Void by Iran

Iran's U.N. Ambassador, Sa'id Raja'i Khorasani, proclaimed in January[68] that conventions, declarations, and resolutions or decisions of international organizations that were contrary to Islam had no validity in the Islamic Republic of Iran.[69] The Universal Declaration of Human Rights, which represented secular understanding of the Judeo-Christian tradition, could not be implemented by Muslims and did not accord with the system of values recognized by the Islamic Republic of Iran[70]; his country would therefore not hesitate

---

67. Ibid.

68. See "Iran Will Never Be Reconciled with Enemies of the Islamic Revolution," BBC Summary of World Broadcasts, Jan. 28, 1993, available in LEXIS, Nexis Library, BBCSWB File.

69. See "Final Report on the Situation of Human Rights in the Islamic Republic of Iran by the Special Representative of the Commission on Human Rights, Mr. Reynaldo Galindo Pohl, pursuant to Commission Resolution 1992/67 of 4 March 1992," U.N. GAOR, Hum.Rts.Comm., 49th Sess., Agenda Item 12, U.N.Doc. E/CN.4/1993/41 (1993).

70. See Imam [Ruhollah] Khomeini, "Islam and Revolution: Writings and Declarations of Imam Khomeini" (1991), 27–166 (explaining Khomeini's own distinctive theory of government by the faqui, or Islamic jurist).

ISLAMIC DIVINE LAW'S (SHARIA) CAPITAL PUNISHMENT

to violate its provisions, since it had to choose between violating the divine law[71] of the country and violating secular conventions.[72]

The Iranian Revolution uniquely demonstrates the clash of cultures between resurgent Islam and Western conception of human rights. The Iranian Revolution, for instance, dispensed with the old Iranian Penal Code, first drafted by a French jurist, heavily drawn from French civil law.[73] Because judges decide "Allah's will" based on sources such as the Qur'an, appeals are considered unnecessary. Some exceptions are made in criminal cases, however, but none in civil cases.[74] Many "secular" lawyers and judges, however, supported the Iranian revolution, not because of religious loyalty[75] but disdain for monarchy.[76]

---

71. See Federal Research Division, Library of Congress, "Iran: A Country Study" (4th ed. 1989), 195-203 (detailing Khomeini's particular system of Islamic government).

72. U.N.Doc. A/C.3/39/SR.65, ¶ 95 (1984); Ann Elizabeth Mayer, "Universal Versus Islamic Human Rights: A Clash of Cultures or a Clash with a Construct?" 15 *MICH. J. INT'L. L.* (1994): 307, 364.

73. S.H. Amin, *Middle East Legal Systems* (1985), 57.

74. Nader Entessar, "Criminal Law and the Legal System in Revolutionary Iran," 8 *B.C. Third World L.J.* (1988): 99. See generally Muhammad Hamdidullah, "Sources of Islamic Law—A New Approach." *Islamic Quarterly* vol. 1 (1954): 205; see generally Ahmad Hasan, "The Sources of Islamic Law" in *Studies in Islamic Law, Religion and Society* (ed. H.S. Bhatia, 1989), 49; see generally Jadulhaqq Ali Jadulhaqq, "The Islamic Shari'a: An Eternal Legislative Source" in *Arab Comparative & Commercial Law* vol. 1 (1987), 111; see generally Muhammad Hashim Kamali, "Source, Nature and Objectives of Shari'ah" *Islamic Quarterly* vol. 33 (1989): 63; see generally W. Wyatt Payne, "The Sources of Mohammedan Law," *American Law Review* 48 (1914): 884; see generally George N. Sfeir, "Source of Law and the Issue of Legitimacy and Rights," *The Middle East Journal* 42 (1988): 436; see generally Hassan Farooq A. "The Sources of Islamic Law," *American Society of International Law: Proceedings of the 76th Annual Meeting* (1982): 65 ; see generally Ahmad bin Mohammed Ibrahim, *Sources of Development of Muslim Law* (1965).

75. Tayyab Mahmud, "Freedom of Religion & Religious Minorities in Pakistan: A Study of Judicial Practice," 19 *FORDHAM INT'L.J.* (October 1995): 40; M. Nadeem Ahmad Siddiq, "Enforced Apostasy: Zaheeruddin v. State and the Official Persecution of the Ahmadiyya Community in Pakistan," 14 *LAW & INEQ.* (December 1995): 275.

76. Michael M.J. Fischer, "Legal Postulates in Flux: Justice, Wit, and

INTERNATIONAL LAW AFLOAT ON A SEA OF WORLD RELIGIONS

A Positive Precedent: International Convention Upheld by Law in a Muslim State

Egypt, however, provides an encouraging counter-example to the ideological recalcitrance of post-Khomeini Iran. Egyptian courts, for instance, honored Article 18 of the International Covenant on Civil and Political Rights, which provides for freedom of religion, to which Egypt is a signatory without reservation. The limitation at issue for the Egyptian courts was Article 18, paragraph 3, which permits restrictions on religious expression should public morals or public order warrant.[77]

Thwarted by presidential decree from Nasser in 1960, the Baha'i were forbidden to exercise their religion in temples or even have temples. Some overzealous police officers arrested 51 Baha'i, three of whom were sentenced to three years in jail. On appeal to the Court of Appeals in Cairo, the Court found that article 18(3) of the international covenant, which Egypt had ratified, was binding, so that their sentence was suspended. But the Court upheld the restriction on public expression of their religion, holding that "public order" justified the decree.[78] Contrast, for instance, Khomeini's death decree on Salmon Rushdie in absentia, without any trial, for blasphemy committed outside Iran.[79]

Hierarchy in Iran," in *Law and Islam in the Middle East* (Daisy Hilse Dwyer ed., 1990), 115–16.

77. "The New International Holy Alliance and the Struggle to Appropriate and Censor General Cultural Symbols, Speech, Religious Discrimination, and Blasphemy," 83 *AM. SOC'Y. INT'L L. PROC.* (April 5–8, 1989): 427, 434.

78. Ibid.

79. Yousef M. Ibrahim, "Muslim Edicts Take on New Force," *New York Times*, February 12, 1995, A14; "The New International Holy Alliance and the Struggle to Appropriate and Censor General Cultural Symbols, Speech, Religious Discrimination, and Blasphemy," 83 *AM. SOC'Y. INT'L L. PROC.* (April 5–8, 1989): 427, 435; Kimberly Younce Schooley, "Cultural Sovereignty, Islam, and Human Rights—Toward a Communitarian Revision," 25 *CUMB. L. REV.* (1994–95): 651.

ISLAMIC DIVINE LAW'S (SHARIA) CAPITAL PUNISHMENT

Legislative Proposals to Crack the Door to Religious Liberty

The Expatriation Option—Non-Muslims Are, Under Reasonable Terms, Deported

The expatriation option involves deportation. Although Article 28 establishes "no Kuwaiti may be deported from Kuwait," deportation of non-citizens of Kuwait is not uncommon. In April 1995, for instance, the Kuwaiti press reported that since the liberation, over 24,000 Bedoons had been issued expulsion orders.[80] After the Gulf War, 250,000 Palestinians were expelled from Kuwait.[81]

Before the mid-1980s, Bedoons had partial freedom to travel (unlike citizens with full freedom to travel) through laissez passer, commonly called Article 17 passports. These temporary passports expired in one year or one round trip abroad, whichever came first. Although Bedoons comprised the overwhelming majority of police and over 90 percent of the enlisted army serviceman (none were officers), in the fall of 1985, Bedoons were singled out by the minister of the Interior, Shaikh Slaem al-Sabah, to be driven out of the country. Although the Bedoons in the military fought the Iraqi invaders, some accused the Bedoons, who are of original Iraqi extraction, of collaborating with the invaders. Others argued that the Kuwaiti military whitewashed itself by claiming the Bedoons as their scapegoats. Passports were no longer issued to Bedoons except for government-approved medical treatment or for one-way travel.[82]

One former Bedoon POW from the Iraqi invasion reported his tragic experience, evidencing one graphic episode in Kuwait's human rights record:

---

80. "Human Rights Watch, The Bedoons of Kuwait—Citizens without Citizenship" (1995), 18.

81. See Ann M. Lesch, "Palestinians in Kuwait," 20(4) *J. PALESTINE STUD.* (1991): 42, 53.

82. Human Rights Watch, "The Bedoons of Kuwait," 19. Since February 1991, drivers licenses and public education have been denied the Bedoons. Human Rights Watch, "The Bedoons of Kuwait," 20.

> (O)ur Iraqi jailers treated us the same; at first they tried to separate Bedoons and treat them better, but the Bedoon POWs refused the preferential treatment. We could have escaped or received better treatment if we had said we were not Kuwaiti. Before we were taken to Iraq, we were kept at the Juvenile Detention Facility [in Kuwait] and the Iraqis asked who was Bedoon; they would have let them go. They [the Bedoons] wouldn't say it; they wanted the same fate as the rest of the Kuwaitis. We celebrated Kuwait's liberation but were shocked at how we were received. Yet you hear many people talk only about those who collaborated.[83]

Actually, Bedoon enlisted men were ordered to resist the Iraqi invaders, many of whom died, while top officers, including the Chief of Staff and his deputy, fled.[84]

Accordingly, deportation is not an unreasonable option for converts from Islam, especially to avoid execution.

The Dispatriation Option—Non-Muslims Are No Longer Under Religious Law and Judiciaries but Allowed into an Internal Apartheid Zone, Designated "International," Allowing for Free Speech

The internal apartheid option involves a designated free zone within Kuwait, perhaps in the section of Kuwait City, where business nerve centers, hotels, and foreign-owned businesses are most dense, permitting a free interchange of religious ideas. Converts from Islam could be allowed to move into the international zone, reside, and be employed there without molestation. A quasi-quarantine could limit entrance to the international apartheid zone to those with non-Islamic foreign passports or visas. If respectability motivates the components in the Kuwaiti Constitution, such as Article 35, issuance of visas for Kuwaiti citizens and resident

---

83. Human Rights Watch interview, Kuwait, January 1994.
84. Human Rights Watch interview, Kuwait, December 1993.

ISLAMIC DIVINE LAW'S (SHARIA) CAPITAL PUNISHMENT

aliens seeking religious asylum in the international apartheid zone would enhance credibility more than words without effect.

CONCLUSION

Reuters' report on January 30, 1997, that Hussein had converted back to Islam does not render the issue of shari'a's capital punishment upon apostates moot. Many "Robert Husseins" have come before, many are present now, and many more will arise. The burden of this article is not that Hussein adhere to any particular religion, but that the fundamental human right of liberty of conscience become a reality in a nation for which the U.S. has invested its own lifeblood.

Many have sought to use Hussein to put a face on the discrimination that Christians endure in Muslim countries, and the conversion of Hussein back to Islam may have removed that face. But nevertheless, the right of Hussein to seek truth for himself without government interference or penal sanctions is an inviolable principle.

Perhaps the most eloquent appeal for an international apartheid zone within Kuwait allowing for religious liberty is Article X of the Universal Islamic Declaration of Human Rights:

> Article X, "Rights of Minorities": . . . In a Muslim country, religious minorities shall have the choice to be governed in respect of their civil and personal matters by Islamic Law or by their own laws.

Application of Article X in an apartheid zone in Kuwait need not involve a change of shari'a dress standards, entertainment and media codes, sexual ethics, or other social mores. Rather, Article X could apply only to the public expression within the zone of

CONCLUSION

different religious beliefs. Of course, Islamic apologists and missionaries could make the apartheid zone their sphere of ministry, seeking to intellectually persuade rather than externally coerce foreigners, resident aliens, and Kuwaiti citizens who seek religious asylum. A free market of religious ideas in a designated area of Kuwait would not threaten the established clerical and political order, but rather demonstrate that the established order in Kuwait has matured to the point that they accept the inviolable principle that conscience is sacred.[1]

---

1. House, H. W. (2014). The Robert Hussein Case and Its Implications for American Foreign Policy. In *The Robert Hussein Case: Its Ramifications for U.S.-Kuwaiti Relations and International Law* (pp. 2–111). Charleston, SC: George J. Gatgounis.

www.ingramcontent.com/pod-product-compliance
Lightning Source LLC
Chambersburg PA
CBHW070512090426
42735CB00012B/2745